Microsoft®
Publisher 2000
Illustrated Introductory

Elizabeth Eisner Reding

COURSE
TECHNOLOGY

Thomson Learning™

ONE MAIN STREET, CAMBRIDGE, MA 02142

Australia • Canada • Denmark • Japan • Mexico • New Zealand • Philippines
Puerto Rico • Singapore • South Africa • Spain • United Kingdom • United States

Microsoft® Publisher 2000—Illustrated Introductory

is published by Course Technology

Senior Product Manager:	Kathryn Schooling
Product Manager:	Rebecca VanEsselstine
Production Editor:	Christine Spillett
Developmental Editor:	Rachel Biheller Bunin
Composition House:	GEX, Inc.
QA Manuscript Reviewers:	Alex White, John Freitas, Johnathan Greacen, Jeff Schwartz
Text Designer:	Joseph Lee, Joseph Lee Designs
Cover Designer:	Doug Goodman, Doug Goodman Designs

For more information contact:

Course Technology
One Main Street
Cambridge, MA 02142
or find us on the World Wide Web at: www.course.com

ISBN 0-7600-6366-4

Printed in the United States of America

6 7 8 9 BM 04 03 02

Exciting New Products

Enhance Any Illustrated Text with these Exciting Products!
Course CBT

Enhance your students' Office 2000 classroom learning experience with self-paced computer-based training (CBT) on CD-ROM. Course CBT engages students with interactive multimedia and hands-on simulations that reinforce and complement the concepts and skills covered in the textbook. All the content is aligned with the MOUS (Microsoft Office User Specialist) program, making it a great preparation tool for the certification exams. Course CBT also includes an extensive pre-assessment exam that automatically generates a "custom learning path" through the course that highlights only the topics students need to practice. It also includes a complete post-assessment exam that test students' mastery of the skills covered.

Sam 2000

How well do your students *really* know Microsoft Office? Sam 2000 is a performance-based testing program that measures students' proficiency in Microsoft Office 2000. You can use Sam 2000 to place students into or out of courses, monitor their performance throughout a course, and help prepare them for the MOUS certification exams.

Create Your Ideal Course Package with CourseKits™

If one book doesn't offer all the coverage you need, create a course package that does. With Course Technology's CourseKits—our mix-and-match approach to selecting texts—you have the freedom to combine products from more than one series. When you choose any two or more Course Technology products for one course, we'll discount the price and package them together so your students can pick up one convenient bundle at the bookstore.

For more information about any of these offerings or other Course Technology products, contact your sales representative or visit our web site at:

www.course.com

Preface

Welcome to *Microsoft Publisher 2000 – Illustrated Introductory.* This highly visual book offers users a hands-on introduction to Publisher 2000 and also serves as an excellent reference for future use.

▶ Organization and Coverage

This text is organized into eight sections as illustrated by the brightly colored tabs on the sides and tops of the pages. In these units students learn how to plan and design a publication, format text, work with art, create Web pages, and use the Publisher Catalog to create publications. They also learn how to define and use styles, work with multiple pages, and enhance a publication with special features.

▶ About this Approach

What makes the Illustrated approach so effective at teaching software skills? It's quite simple. Each skill is presented on two facing pages, with the step-by-step instructions on the left page, and large screen illustrations on the right. Students can focus on a single skill without having to turn the page. This unique design makes information extremely accessible and easy to absorb, and provides a great reference for after the course is over. This hands-on approach also makes it ideal for both self-paced or instructor-led classes.

Each lesson, or "information display," contains the following elements:

Each 2-page spread focuses on a single skill.

Concise text that introduces the basic principles discussed in the lesson. Procedures are easier to learn when concepts fit into a framework.

Unit D — Publisher 2000

Aligning and Grouping Images

Once you have inserted clip art, you can align multiple images so that the layout of the publication looks professionally designed. Artwork can be aligned from left to right or from top to bottom. Images can also be arranged in groups. A group makes it easy to move several pieces of art as one unit. ➤ Mary wants to make sure the three images on the page are precisely lined up. Then she will move them as a group.

Steps

1. **Press and hold [Shift], click the right image, click the left image, then release [Shift]**
   All three images should be selected, as shown in Figure D-10. You can use the shortcut menu to line up the objects.

2. **Place the pointer over one of the images, right-click the objects, then click Align Objects**
   The Align Objects dialog box opens, as shown in Figure D-11. You want the objects lined up top to bottom along their centers.

   QuickTip
   You can also line up objects by selecting the objects, clicking Arrange on the menu bar, then clicking Align Objects.

3. **Click the Top to bottom Centers option button, then click OK**
   Now that the images are all perfectly lined up, you can group them to make sure the alignment is preserved when you move them.

4. **Click the Group Objects button**
   The three selected objects are transformed into a single selected object.

5. **Drag the selected grouped object so that the lower edge of the frame is at 6½" V**
   Compare your work with Figure D-12. You don't always want to retain the group; you can always regroup later.

   QuickTip
   You can move selected grouped or ungrouped objects by pressing an arrow key (on the keyboard) while pressing and holding [Alt].

6. **Click the Ungroup Objects button, then press [F9]**
   Save your work.

7. **Click the Save button on the Standard toolbar**

CLUES TO USE
Scanning artwork

If you have a favorite photo or piece of artwork that does not exist in electronic form, you can convert it to a digital computer file with a scanner. A variety of scanners are available, in either a hand-held or flatbed format. You can scan text, line art, or full-color images with amazing accuracy, enabling you to use virtually any image as clip art. Every scanner comes with its own easy-to-use imaging software. Publisher also lets you scan directly into a publication by clicking Insert on the menu bar, pointing to Picture, then clicking Scanner or Camera. The Picture menu commands appear dimmed unless a scanner or camera is installed on the computer.

▶ 80 | WORKING WITH ART

QuickTips as well as troubleshooting advice right where you need it — next to the step itself.

Clear step-by-step directions, with what students are to type in green. When students follow the numbered steps, they quickly learn how each procedure is performed and what the results will be.

Clues to Use boxes provide concise information that either expands on one component of the major lesson skill or describes an independent task that is in some way related to the major lesson skill.

Every lesson features large-size, full-color representations of what the students' screen should look like after completing the numbered steps.

Brightly colored tabs indicate which section of the book you are in. Useful for finding your place within the book and for referencing information from the index.

FIGURE D-10: All three images selected

ag line

This is a good place to mention the purpose of the fund-raiser, individuals or organizations that will be helped, potential changes or benefits to the community, and fund-raising goals, such as dollar amounts. Be sure to convey the importance of your cause and highlight the benefits of being a supporter or participant.

m by
team.

5 555

Click to group individual objects

FIGURE D-11: Align Objects dialog box

Align Objects

Left to right
- No change
- Left edges
- Centers
- Right edges

Top to bottom
- No change
- Top edges
- Centers
- Bottom edges

Sample

No change

Sample shows selected alignment option

Alignment options

Align along margins

Design Tip
Use the Align Along Margins check box to align objects with the margins of the page, or to center the objects on the page.

OK   Cancel   Apply

TABLE D-1: Common graphic image formats

graphic image	extension	graphic image	extension
Bitmap	.BMP	Tagged Image File Format	.TIF
PC Paintbrush	.PCX	JPEG Picture Format	.JPG or .JPEG
Graphics Interchange Format	.GIF	Windows Metafile	.WMF
Encapsulated PostScript	.EPS	CorelDraw	.CDR

Publisher 2000

Quickly accessible summaries of key terms, toolbar buttons, or keyboard alternatives connected with the lesson material. Students can refer easily to this information when working on their own projects at a later time.

Additional Features

The two-page lesson format featured in this book provides the new user with a powerful learning experience. Additionally, this book contains the following features:

▶ **Real-World Case**

The case study used throughout the textbook, a fictitious company called Image Masters, is designed to be "real-world" in nature and introduces the kinds of activities that students will encounter when working with Publisher. With a real-world case, the process of solving problems will be more meaningful to students.

▶ **End of Unit Material**

Each unit concludes with a Concepts Review that tests students' understanding of what they learned in the unit. The Concepts Review is followed by a Skills Review, which provides students with additional hands-on practice of the skills they learned in the unit. The Skills Review is followed by Independent Challenges, which pose case problems for students to solve. The Independent Challenges allow students to learn by exploring and to develop critical thinking skills. At least one Independent Challenge in each unit asks students to use the World Wide Web to solve the problem as indicated by a Web Work icon. Visual Workshops that follow the Independent Challenges in the later units help students to develop critical thinking skills. Students are shown completed documents and are asked to recreate them from scratch.

Instructor's Resource Kit

The Instructor's Resource Kit is Course Technology's way of putting the resources and information needed to teach and learn effectively into your hands. With an integrated array of teaching and learning tools that offers you and your students a broad range of technology-based instructional options, we believe this kit represents the highest quality and most cutting edge resources available to instructors today. Many of these resources are available at www.course.com. The resources available with this book are:

Course Test Manager Designed by Course Technology, this Windows-based software helps instructors design, administer, and print tests and pre-tests. A full-featured program, Course Test Manager also has an online testing component that allows students to take tests at the computer and have their exams automatically graded.

Instructor's Manual Available as an electronic file, the Instructor's Manual is quality-assurance tested and includes unit overviews, detailed lecture topics for each unit with teaching tips, an Upgrader's Guide, solutions to all lessons and end-of-unit material, and extra Independent Challenges. The Instructor's Manual is available on the Instructor's Resource Kit CD-ROM or you can download it from www.course.com.

Course Faculty Online Companion You can browse this textbook's password-protected site to obtain the Instructor's Manual, Solution Files, Project Files, and any updates to the text. Contact your Customer Service Representative for the site address and password.

Project Files Project Files contain all of the data that students will use to complete the lessons and end-of-unit material. A Readme file includes instructions for using the files. Adopters of this text are granted the right to install the Project Files on any standalone computer or network. The Project Files are available on the Instructor's Resource Kit CD-ROM, the Review Pack, and can also be downloaded from www.course.com.

Solution Files Solution Files contain every file students are asked to create or modify in the lessons and end-of-unit material. A Help file on the Instructor's Resource Kit includes information for using the Solution Files.

Figure Files The figures in the text are provided on the Instructor's Resourse Kit CD to help illustrate key topics or concepts. Instructors can create traditional overhead transparencies by printing the figure files. Or they can create electronic slide shows by using the figures in a presentation program such as PowerPoint.

Student Online Companion This book features its own Online Companion where students can go to access Web sites that will help them complete the Webwork Independent Challenges. Because the Web is constantly changing, the Student Online Companion will provide the reader with current updates regarding links referenced in the book

WebCT WebCT is a tool used to create Web-based educational environments and also uses WWW browsers as the interface for the course-building environment. The site is hosted on your school campus, allowing complete control over the information. WebCT has its own internal communication system, offering internal e-mail, a Bulletin Board, and a Chat room.

Course Technology offers pre-existing supplemental information to help in your WebCT class creation, such as a suggested Syllabus, Lecture Notes, Figures in the Book/Course Presenter, Student Downloads, and Test Banks in which you can schedule an exam, create reports, and more.

Brief Contents

Contents

Publisher 2000

Contents

Working with Art   73

Contents

Enhancing a Publication   97

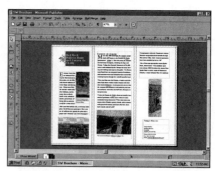

Working with Multiple Pages

Contents

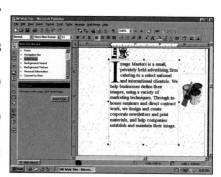

Working on the Web   169

Contents

Unit
A

Getting
Started with Microsoft Publisher 2000

Objectives

- ► Define publication software
- ► Start Publisher 2000
- ► View the Publisher window
- ► Open and save a publication
- ► Enter text in a frame
- ► View and print a publication
- ► Get Help and change Personal Information
- ► Close a publication and exit Publisher

Microsoft Publisher 2000 is a popular desktop publishing program that operates using the Windows operating system. In this unit, you will learn how to start Publisher and use elements found in the Publisher window and menus. You will also learn how to open and save existing files, enter text in a publication, view and print a publication, use the extensive Help system, and change Personal Information. ➤ Carlos Mendoza is an account executive at Image Masters, a small advertising agency. Carlos will use Publisher to create a flyer announcing the location of the agency's new office.

Defining Publication Software

Publisher is a desktop publishing program. A **desktop publishing** program lets you combine text and graphics, as well as worksheets and charts you may have created in other programs, to produce a document. A document created in Publisher is called a **publication**. Table A-1 contains examples of the types of publications you can create. ━━ Carlos loves using Publisher because he can create a variety of professional-looking publications quickly and easily. The benefits of using Publisher include the ability to:

Details

Create professional publications

Publisher comes with a Catalog that lets you choose the type of publication you want to design, helps you decide on its appearance, and then suggests text and graphic image placement to complete the publication. The **Quick Publication Wizard** creates complete publications that you can modify easily to meet your specific needs.

Use clip art

Artwork not only makes any publication appear more vibrant and interesting, but also helps explain your ideas. Publisher comes with more than 10,000 pieces of artwork that can be incorporated into your publications. In addition, any other personal illustrations and photographs can be imported into the **Clip Gallery** (the artwork organizer), with a scanner or from the Web.

Create logos

Most organizations want a special symbol, shape, or color—or combination of these—to attach a recognizable graphic to their name. This distinctive shape, called a **logo**, can be created using Publisher's Logo Wizard or by designing your own artwork and text. Figure A-1 illustrates a sample flyer created in Publisher that contains a logo formed by combining clip art and text.

Make your work look consistent

Publisher has many tools to help you create consistent publications that have similar design elements. Use **Design sets** to create different types of stylized publications. When creating work from scratch, you might, for example, want to have an information box in the lower-left corner on the back page of all Image Masters flyers. Using rulers and layout guides, you can create grids to help position graphics and text on a page. You can save a publication as a **template**, a special publication that serves as a master for other publications.

Work with multiple pages

Publisher makes it easy to work with multipage publications. Pages can be added, deleted, and moved within a publication. Text that continues on more than one page is connected and flows logically between pages.

Emphasize special text

Any publication looks boring if all the text looks the same, so you should use text styles to express different meanings and convey messages. Use a **pull quote** to set a short statement off to the side, and a **sidebar** to make an important story stand out and grab a reader's attention.

Publish on the Internet

Publisher can be used to create Web pages, using the Web Site Wizard. The **Web Site Wizard** makes it easy to include links and graphics. Page backgrounds and animated GIFs add color and motion to your pages. A **Web Publishing Wizard** helps you make your Web site available to a local network drive or company intranet.

FIGURE A-1: Sample flyer

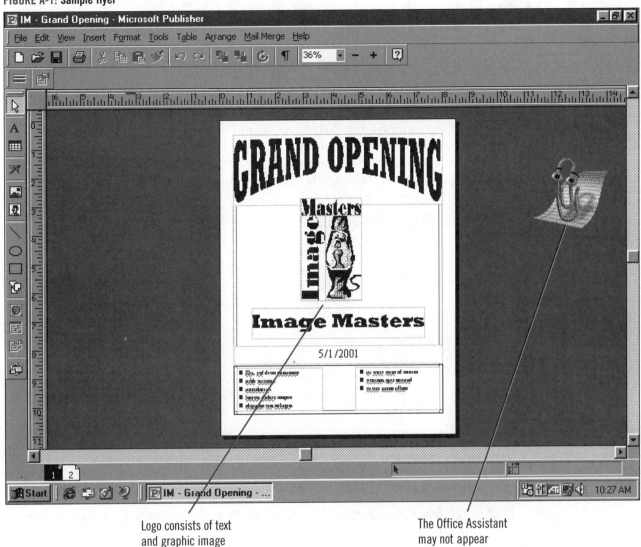

Logo consists of text
and graphic image

The Office Assistant
may not appear

TABLE A-1: Common publications

publication	example
Periodical	Newsletters, booklets
Promotional	Advertisements, flyers, press releases
Informational	Brochures, signs, calendars, forms
Stationery	Letterhead, labels, business cards, envelopes, postcards
Specialty	Banners, airplanes, origami, resumes, award certificates, gift certificates

Publisher 2000

Starting Publisher 2000

To start Publisher, you use the Start button on the taskbar. A slightly different procedure might be required for computers on a network and those that use utility programs that enhance Windows. If you need assistance, ask your instructor or technical support person for help. When you start Publisher, the computer displays the Catalog. This dialog box lets you select a Wizard, select a publication by design, open an existing publication, or start with a blank page. Carlos begins by starting Publisher, and he opens a blank full-page publication.

1. Locate the **Start button** 🏁Start on the taskbar
The Start button is on the left side of the taskbar and is used to start programs on your computer.

QuickTip

Microsoft Publisher 2000 can be used with Windows 95 or higher versions.

2. Click the **Start button** 🏁Start
Microsoft Publisher is located in the Programs group, located at the top of the Start menu, as shown in Figure A-2.

3. Point to **Programs**
All the programs on your computer, including Microsoft Publisher, can be found in this area of the Start menu. You can see the Microsoft Publisher icon and other Microsoft programs, as shown in Figure A-3. Your Programs menu might look different, depending on the programs installed on your computer.

Trouble?

If you don't see the Microsoft Publisher icon, look in a folder called Microsoft Office or Office 2000.

4. Click the **Microsoft Publisher program icon** 🅿
Publisher opens and the Catalog dialog box opens. This dialog box has three tabs: Publications by Wizard, Publications by Design, and Blank Publications. You decide to open a blank full-page publication.

5. Click the **Blank Publications tab**, click **Full Page** if necessary, then click **Create**
A blank full-page publication displays on the screen.

6. Click the **Hide Wizard button** ▼ Hide Wizard located just above the Start button
The Quick Publication Wizard is no longer visible. In the next lesson, you will familiarize yourself with the elements of the Publisher window.

FIGURE A-2: Start menu

Microsoft Publisher located in this group

Click here to open Start menu

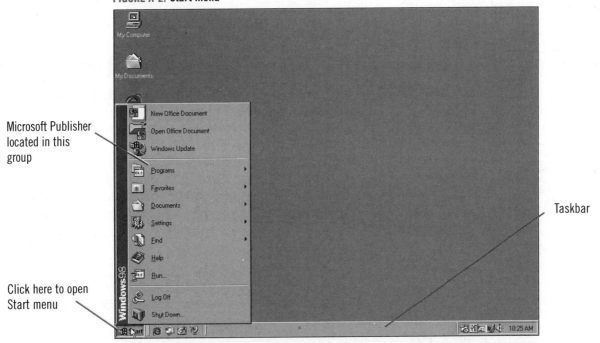

Taskbar

FIGURE A-3: Programs available on your computer

Microsoft Publisher program icon

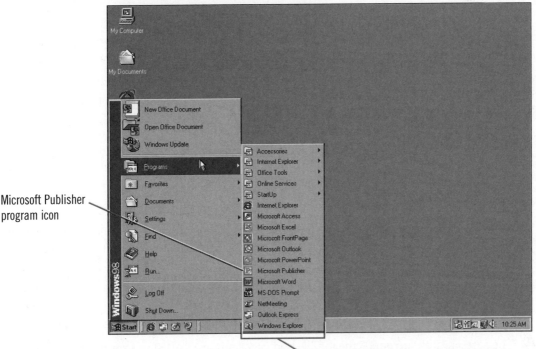

List of available programs might vary

Making use of wizards

A Wizard is a series of dialog boxes that leads you through a particular process. In Publisher, a wizard can help you create a publication. Publisher 2000 includes the Quick Publication Wizard that helps you create a variety of single-page publications easily. The Catalog Wizard contains more than 20 publication templates that help you create multipage publications such as newsletters and booklets. As you proceed through a wizard, you can select many options—such as color schemes and personal information sets. The choices you make personalize your publication, and any text or graphics in the resulting publication can always be changed later.

Publisher 2000

Publisher 2000

Viewing the Publisher Window

The area where a new or existing publication appears is called the **workspace**. The workspace is where you actually work on a publication, and each page within a publication is viewed here. Unlike most other programs, Publisher allows only one publication to be open at a time. Carlos takes some time to familiarize himself with the Publisher workspace and its elements before he works on the flyer. Compare the descriptions below to Figure A-4.

 The **title bar** displays the program name (Microsoft Publisher) and the filename of the open publication (in this case, Unsaved Publication because the file has not yet been named and saved). The title bar also contains a control menu box, a Close button, and resizing buttons.

 The **menu bar** contains menus from which you choose Publisher commands. As with all Windows programs, you can choose a menu command by clicking it with the mouse or by pressing [Alt] plus the underlined letter in the menu name. A menu containing a down arrow at its lower edge contains additional commands. To see these commands, click the down arrow, or wait several seconds, and the commands will appear. Once you select a previously hidden command, it will appear on the menu from that point on.

 The **toolbars** contain buttons for frequently used Publisher commands. The **Standard toolbar** is located just below the menu bar and contains buttons corresponding to the most frequently used Publisher features. Place the pointer over each button to display the ScreenTip to see what each button does. To select a button, simply click it with the left mouse button. The face of any button has a graphic representation of its function; for instance, the Print button has a printer on its face.

 Horizontal and vertical **rulers** are displayed beneath the toolbars and to the left of the workspace. Rulers help you precisely measure the size of objects as well as place objects in precise locations on a page. These rulers also can be moved from the edge of the workspace to a more convenient position on the page. Your rulers may have different beginning and ending numbers, depending on the size of your monitor, the resolution of your display, and the positioning of the page on the workspace.

 The **workspace page** contains the currently displayed page.

 Page icons are used to navigate from page to page. Click the icon for the page you want to view. In a multipage publication, an icon is displayed for each page; the icon for the currently displayed page appears in black.

 The **status bar** is located at the bottom of the Publisher window. The left side of the status bar displays page icons and may contain a Show or Hide Wizard button. The right side of the status bar shows the object status, which includes the size and position of selected objects.

 The **scratch area** surrounds the publication page and can be used to store objects.

FIGURE A-4: Blank publication

Control menu box

Title bar

Menu bar

Objects toolbar

Status bar

Click to display Wizard

Page icons help you select and move to pages

Rulers

Object position

Scratch area/workspace

System tray contains peripheral icons; yours will be different

Close window button

Resizing buttons

Standard toolbar

Vertical scroll bar

Workspace page

Object size

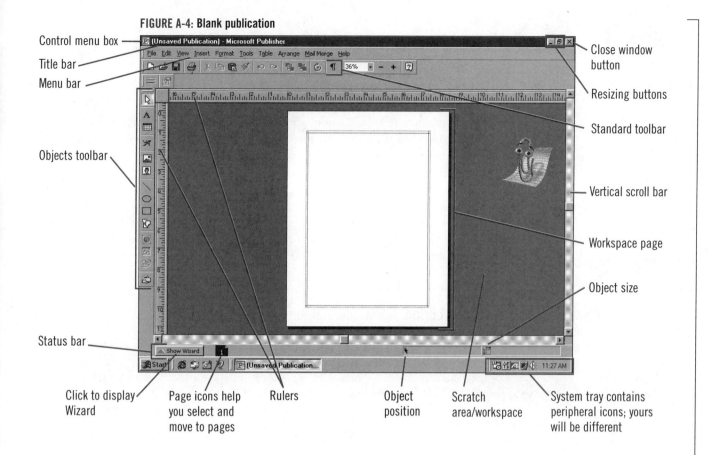

Publisher 2000

Publisher 2000

Opening and Saving a Publication

Often a project is completed in stages: you might start working on a publication and then stop to do other work or take a break. Later, you'll resume working and complete it. Sometimes it's more efficient to create a new publication by modifying one that already exists. This approach saves you from having to re-create existing information. Throughout this book, you will be instructed to open a file from your Project Disk, use the Save As command to create a copy of the file with a new name, and then modify the new file by following the lesson steps. Saving the files with new names keeps your original Project Disk files intact in case you have to start the lesson over again, or you wish to repeat an exercise. ◤ Carlos started the Image Masters flyer and is ready to finish it. He opens the Image Masters flyer, then uses the Save As command to create a copy of the file with a new name.

Steps 1 2 3 4

QuickTip

If you click the Preview button on the Views palette, the Preview pane shows a reduced image of the selected publication.

1. Click the **Open button** 🖻 on the Standard toolbar
The Open Publication dialog box opens. See Figure A-5.

2. Click the **Look in list arrow**
A list of the available drives appears. The files that you need for these lessons are located on your Project Disk. In these lessons we assume your Project Disk is in drive A.

3. Click **3½ Floppy (A:)**
A list of the files on your Project Disk appears.

Trouble?

Publisher may display a message that the printer cannot be initialized. Click OK to change to your default printer.

4. Click the file **PUB A-1**, then click **Open**
The file PUB A-1 opens. You could also double-click the filename to open the file. To create and save a copy of this file with a new name, you use the Save As command.

5. Click **File** on the menu bar, then click **Save As**
The Save As dialog box opens.

6. Make sure the **Save in list box** displays the drive containing your Project Disk
You should save all your files to your Project Disk, unless instructed otherwise.

7. Select the current filename in the File name text box, if necessary, then type **Grand Opening flyer**
See Figure A-6.

QuickTip

Use the Save As command to create a new publication from an existing one. Use the Save command to store any changes made to an existing file on your disk.

8. Click **Save**
The Save As dialog box closes, the file PUB A-1 closes, and a duplicate file named Grand Opening flyer is now open, as shown in Figure A-7. To save the publication in the future, you can click File on the menu bar, then click Save, or click the Save button on the Standard toolbar.

FIGURE A-5: Open Publication dialog box

Click to display a list of available drives

Available files and folders appear here

FIGURE A-6: Save As dialog box

Current drive or folder

Your list of files might be different

Type the new filename here

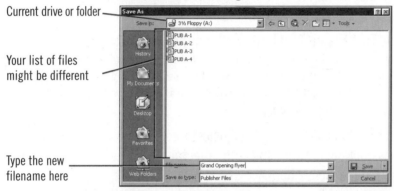

FIGURE A-7: Grand Opening flyer publication

Publication name is displayed in title bar

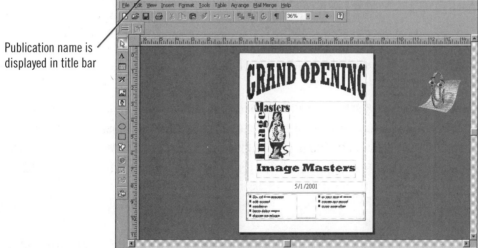

Using dialog box views

You may notice that the information displayed in Open and Save As dialog boxes varies depending on the currently selected View. There are four Views: List, Details, Properties, and Preview. The List View displays the names of the contents of a given folder. The Details View displays the same information as the List View, but includes the size, the last date and time the file was saved, and the file type. The Properties View displays detailed information on the file size and when it was modified (document properties are not always available). The Preview View displays a thumbnail image of the file (previews are not always available). Select a View based on the type of information you need by clicking the Views list arrow in a dialog box, and then click the View you want.

Entering Text in a Frame

In word processing, text is entered directly on a page. In desktop publishing, however, text is a small part of any publication because graphic objects contribute significantly to the layout. Rather than enter text beginning at a margin's edge, you enter text in a publication within a text frame. A text frame is an object into which text is typed. Any frame can be moved, resized, and connected to other frames. An object can be selected by clicking anywhere within it. When an object is selected, small (usually black) squares called **handles** appear around its perimeter. A frame can contain text, graphics, tables, and other frames. Carlos enters some additional text needed within the flyer.

Steps

1. Click the **Text Frame Tool button** A on the Objects toolbar

The Text Frame tool creates a text frame. The pointer changes to ┼. You want to create a rectangular text frame that is slightly smaller than the Image Masters logo and located to its right. You use the object coordinates (displayed in inches in the status bar) to size and position the object with precision.

2. Position the ┼ pointer so that the object location is **3.5, 3.25 in.**, press and hold the left mouse button, drag ┼ to create a rectangle whose object size is **3.75 × 2.75 in.**, then release the mouse button

The Formatting toolbar appears. As you drag the object shape, the coordinates on the status bar change to display the object size and the position of the pointer in the workspace. When the mouse button is released, the text frame appears as a selected object surrounded by handles, with the insertion point blinking at the top-left corner, as shown in Figure A-8. Notice that additional buttons appear on the Formatting toolbar. This means that Publisher is ready for you to type text. Before typing the text, however, you decide to use the Zoom feature to make the text readable. Placeholders are often used in publications as reminders of where information should be inserted.

3. Press [F9], type **We are very excited about our new office space. Here, we will be able to offer you services in a more professional atmosphere. Please join us at our Grand Opening celebration on Thursday, October 1, 2001.**, press [Enter] twice, then type **Our new address is Crimson Corner,**, press [Enter], then type **Suite 200, Santa Fe, NM 87501**

You should enlarge the text to make it easier to read. **Point size** is a measurement that determines the height of a character. The text is currently at 10 points; it would be easier to read at 16 points.

4. Drag the I pointer to select all the text in the frame, click the **Font Size list arrow** 12 ▾ on the **Formatting toolbar**, then click **16**

The text in the text frame is shown in Figure A-9. You decide you want to see as much of the publication as possible.

5. Click the **Zoom list arrow** 36% ▾, click **50%**, then click anywhere on the scratch area to deselect the text frame

Although you have more entries to make, you save your work and plan on completing the flyer later.

6. Click the **Save button** 🖫 on the Standard toolbar

It is a good idea to save your work early and often in the creation process, especially before making significant changes to the publication or before printing.

FIGURE A-8: Text frame in publication

Standard toolbar

Formatting toolbar

Text Frame Tool button

Objects toolbar

Text frame

Handles

Placeholder text

Object coordinates for position of selected text frame

Object coordinates for size of selected text frame

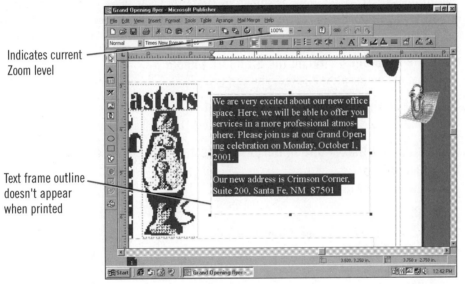

FIGURE A-9: Completed text in text frame

Indicates current Zoom level

Text frame outline doesn't appear when printed

Understanding frames

Frames are used to contain text, pictures (graphic images), or tables. Any frame can be resized or moved, and can also be used in layers. In addition, framed text can be wrapped around a framed object. The advantage to using frames is that contents within the frame can be moved anywhere within a publication. Unlike word processing, in which all text and graphics are placed relative to margins, frames can be moved wherever you want in whatever size you choose. Figure A-10 shows text wrapped around a framed graphic image.

FIGURE A-10: Text wrapped around a picture

Publisher 2000

Viewing and Printing a Publication

When a publication is completed, you can print it to have a paper copy to reference, file, or send to others. You can also print a publication that is not complete, to review it or work on it when you are not at a computer. Before you print a publication, it is good to preview it using the Zoom feature to make sure that it will fit on a page the way you want. Unlike other programs, Publisher doesn't have a special Print Preview feature: you're always viewing the pages exactly the way they'll print. Table A-2 provides printing tips. ✐ Carlos prints a copy of the Image Masters flyer to show to a coworker.

Steps

Trouble?

If a file is sent to print and the printer is off, an error message appears.

1. **Make sure the printer is on and contains paper**
   The Zoom buttons let you check the flyer's overall appearance.

2. **Click the Zoom Out button** [−] **on the Standard toolbar**
   You could also click the Zoom list button, then click 33% or Full Page. The page is displayed within the workspace window, as shown in Figure A-11. If there were multiple pages, you would see additional page icons. To see any additional pages, you can click the displayed page icons.

3. **Click the Save button** [🖫] **on the Standard toolbar**
   Now that the publication is saved, you can print it.

QuickTip

You can also use the Print button [🖨] on the Standard toolbar to print every page in a publication.

4. **Click File on the menu bar, then click Print**
   The Print dialog box opens, as shown in Figure A-12.

5. **Make sure that the All option button is selected, and that 1 appears in the Number of copies text box**
   Now you are ready to print the publication.

6. **Click OK**
   Review the publication to see if it printed as expected.

FIGURE A-11: Whole page in workspace

One page indicates a single-page publication

Zoom Out button

FIGURE A-12: Print dialog box

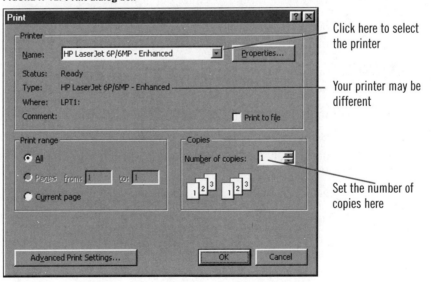

Click here to select the printer

Your printer may be different

Set the number of copies here

TABLE A-2: Publication printing tips

before you print	recommendation
Check the printer	Make sure that the printer is turned on and online, that it has paper, and that there are no error messages or warning signals
Check the printer selection	Use the Printer Name command in the Print dialog box to make sure the correct printer is selected

Publisher 2000

Getting Help and Changing Personal Information

Publisher features an extensive Help system that gives you immediate access to definitions, explanations, and useful tips. The Help system is displayed along the right side of the workspace. When opened, the window can be resized for your comfort, and it can remain on the screen so you can refer to it as you work. ✐ Carlos decides to use Help to find out about Personal Information and how it can be modified.

Trouble?

Once it's hidden, you can display the Office Assistant by clicking the Help button ⛄ on the Standard toolbar.

Trouble?

If necessary, use the scroll bars to see all the information in the Help window, or click the blue links to read additional information.

Trouble?

If the Office Assistant is blocking your view, click the image and drag it to a new location.

1. Click the **Office Assistant**

The Office Assistant Help window opens. Information can be accessed at any time while Publisher is open.
It would be helpful to learn about modifying Personal Information sets.

2. Type **How do I change Personal Information?**, then click **Search**

The Office Assistant displays topics about Personal Information, as seen in Figure A-13.

3. Click **Change information within a Personal Information set**, then read about making modifications to a Personal Information set

The Help window works just like any other window. It can be closed using the Close box, and the Office Assistant can be hidden at any time.

4. Click the **Publisher Help window Close box**, right-click the **Office Assistant**, then click **Hide**

The Office Assistant is hidden. Any Personal Information set can be modified, and the changes can be used in future publications.

5. Click **Edit** on the menu bar, then click **Personal Information**

Modifying a Personal Information set is as easy as replacing existing data with new text.

6. Click **Secondary Business** information set in the Personal Information dialog box

The information displayed is for the current secondary business.

7. Drag ⌶ to select the *current name* in the Name text box, type **Carlos Mendoza**, press **[Tab]**, then refer to Figure A-14 to type the rest of the information in the Personal Information dialog box (including job title, phone numbers, e-mail, and color schemes)

The information set modifications take effect when they have been updated.

8. Click **Update**

FIGURE A-13: Office Assistant Help topics

Click a topic to get more information

Question posed to the Office Assistant

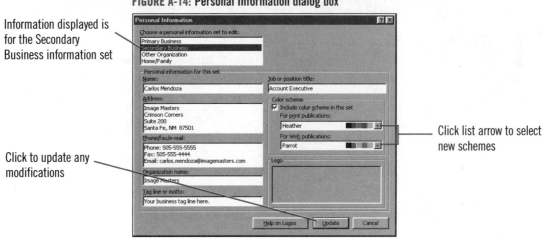

FIGURE A-14: Personal Information dialog box

Information displayed is for the Secondary Business information set

Click to update any modifications

Click list arrow to select new schemes

Using Personal Information sets

Because you probably create publications about yourself, or your business or organization, Publisher makes it easy for you to store frequently used information. This feature—called Personal Information sets—means that you won't have to enter it each time. You can store four Personal Information sets: for your primary and secondary businesses, another organization, and your home or family. The information in the Primary Business set is applied by default, but you can easily apply information in any of the other sets with the click of a button. Figure A-15 shows how the information set is changed in a publication created with a Wizard.

FIGURE A-15: Changing the Personal Information set with a Wizard

Select Personal Information

Click the option button for the set you want to modify

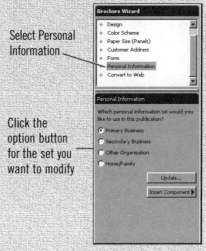

Publisher 2000

Publisher 2000

Closing a Publication and Exiting Publisher

When you have finished working on a publication, you need to save the file and close it. When you have completed all your work in Publisher, you need to exit the program. Closing a file puts away a publication file but leaves Publisher running. Exiting puts away a publication file and returns you to the desktop, where you can choose to run another program. Carlos has finished adding the information to the Image Masters flyer and needs to attend a meeting, so he closes the publication and then exits Publisher.

Steps

1. Click File on the menu bar

The File menu opens. See Figure A-16.

2. Click Close

You could also click the Close button on the title bar instead of choosing File, Close Publication.

3. If asked if you want to save your work, click Yes

Publisher closes the publication and displays a blank publication with the Quick Publication Wizard on the left of your workspace.

QuickTip

To exit Publisher and close an open publication, click the Close button in the upper-right corner of the window. Publisher will prompt you to save any unsaved changes before closing.

4. Click File on the menu bar, then click Exit

You could also double-click the program control menu box to exit the program. Publisher closes, and computer memory is freed up for other computing tasks.

Microsoft Publisher World Wide Web site

You can get even more information by accessing the Microsoft Publisher Web site. This constantly changing site offers tips and how-to information, as well as new developments. By clicking on the blue links, you'll be able to find additional information on this product. Figure A-17 shows the Publisher 2000 Product Overview Web site, although it may look different on your screen, because this site changes often. To find even more information, you can search the Internet (using a search engine such as Yahoo!) for any sites about Microsoft Publisher.

FIGURE A-16: Closing a publication using the File menu

Program control menu box

Close button

Close command

Light-colored menu commands have not yet been used

Exit command

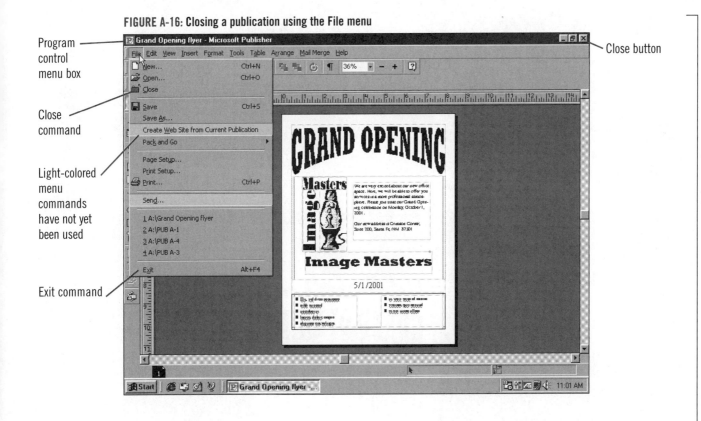

FIGURE A-17: Microsoft Publisher Web site

Site address

Click a link to get more information

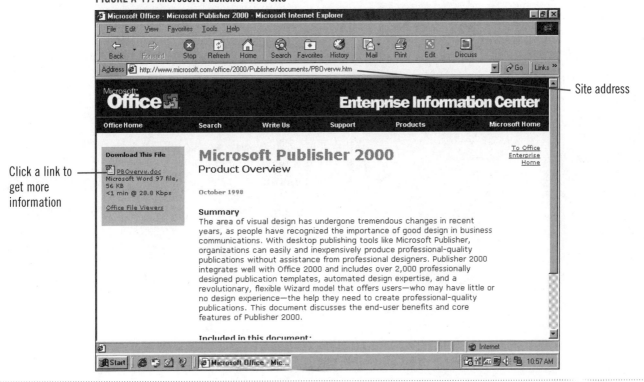

Practice

► Concepts Review

Label each of the elements in the Publisher window shown in Figure A-18.

FIGURE A-18

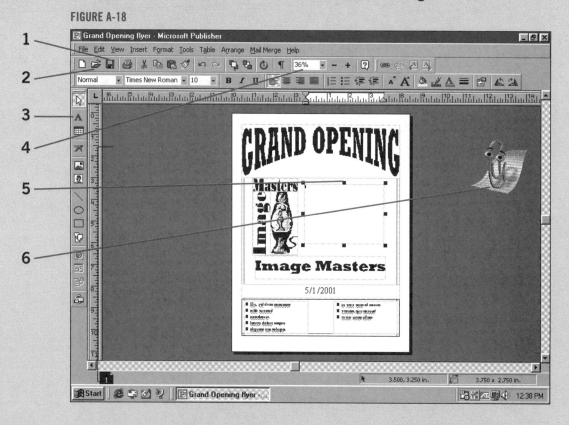

Match each of the terms or buttons with the statement that describes its function.

7. 🖼
8. 💾
9. **Text frame**
10. 🖨
11. **Handles**
12. **Status bar**

a. Used to save a publication on a disk
b. Small black squares surrounding an object
c. Shows size and position of selected object
d. Contains typed text
e. Opens an existing publication
f. Prints every page in the publication

Select the best answer from the list of choices.

13. A document created in Publisher is called a
- **a.** Magazine.
- **b.** Notebook.
- **c.** Publication.
- **d.** Brochure.

14. Which of the following statements about frames is false?
- **a.** They can be moved.
- **b.** They can be resized.
- **c.** They can be inverted.
- **d.** They can be connected to other frames.

15. Which key is pressed to zoom into a selected area?
- **a.** [F8]
- **b.** [F2]
- **c.** [F6]
- **d.** [F9]

16. A template is
- **a.** A special publication that serves as a master for other publications.
- **b.** A short statement placed off to the side to grab a reader's attention.
- **c.** An online artwork organizer.
- **d.** A distinctive shape in a publication.

17. Frames are used to contain
- **a.** Text.
- **b.** Pictures.
- **c.** Tables.
- **d.** All of the above.

18. Which button is used to create a text box?
- **a.**
- **b.**
- **c.**
- **d.**

19. Which feature is used to enlarge a page?
- **a.** Magnify
- **b.** Enlarge
- **c.** Amplify
- **d.** Zoom In

20. Each of the following is found in the status bar, *except*
    a. A selected object's position.
    b. The name of the current publication.
    c. Page icons.
    d. A selected object's size.

21. The four sets of information for use in publications are called
    a. Priority information sets.
    b. Personalized info selection.
    c. Personal information sets.
    d. Personal information selection.

▶ Skills Review

1. **Start Publisher 2000.**
    a. Start Publisher.
    b. Open a blank full page.
    c. Try to identify as many elements in the Publisher window as you can without referring to the unit material.

2. **Open and save a publication.**
    a. Open the file PUB A-2. If you get a message to initialize the default printer, click OK.
    b. Save the publication as Sample Business Card.

3. **Enter text in a frame.**
    a. Create a text frame for your name, using Figure A-19 as a guide. (Substitute your own name for the Course Technology placeholder.) Use a 16-point text size.
    b. Create a text frame for your address, using Figure A-19 as a guide. (Substitute your own address for the Course Technology placeholder.) Use a 14-point text size.
    c. Save the publication.

FIGURE A-19

4. **View and print a publication.**
   a. Zoom out.
   b. Zoom in until all text is readable.
   c. Print one copy of the publication.

5. **Get Help and change Personal Information.**
   a. If necessary, use the button on the Standard toolbar to display the Office Assistant.
   b. Click the Office Assistant.
   c. Find information on the Publisher Catalog. (*Hint*: Ask the Assistant, "What is the Catalog?")
   d. Click the Print button above the Help window to print the information you find.
   e. Close the Help window.
   f. Hide the Office Assistant.
   g. Open the Personal Information dialog box.
   h. Select the Secondary Business information set.
   i. Change the tag line for the Secondary Business to "We make you look your best."

6. **Close the publication and exit Publisher.**
   a. Close your publication.
   b. Exit Publisher.

▶ Independent Challenges

1. The Publisher Help feature provides definitions, explanations, procedures, and other helpful information. It also provides examples and demonstrations to show how Publisher features work. Topics include elements such as the workspace, frames, and selecting objects, as well as detailed information about Publisher commands and options.

From an existing publication, explore Help using the Office Assistant. Find out how to add a page to a publication. Print out the information.

2. Desktop publishing programs can be used to create many types of publications. Some examples of the ways Publisher can be used are discussed at the beginning of this unit. Publisher has many applications within the classroom. If you were teaching a class, how could you use Publisher to your advantage as a teaching aid?

   To complete this independent challenge:

a. Think of three types of publications you could create with Publisher that would be effective within a classroom.

b. Sketch a sample of each publication.

c. Open a blank publication for each sample. Using text frames, re-create your sketches. (These publications don't need to be fancy; they can just contain text frames.) Your three publications should be named Suggestion 1, Suggestion 2, and Suggestion 3.

d. In a separate blank publication, use text frames to explain why each of your suggestions would be an effective use of Publisher. Name this publication Explanation.

e. Be sure to include your name in each Publication, then print each one.

3. You've been selected as the Image Masters Employee of the Month. You're being honored because you always come up with creative ways of accomplishing tasks. When you were given your award, you were asked for ways to improve the certificate. To complete the certificate, more text is needed.

To complete this independent challenge:

a. Start Publisher if necessary, then open the file PUB A-3 and save it as IM-Award.

b. Use Zoom as needed. In the space above the Name of Recipient placeholder, insert a text frame that contains an explanation of why you are being given this award.

c. Replace the Name of Recipient placeholder with your own name.

d. Print the final publication.

e. Save your work.

f. Close the publication, exit Publisher.

4. The World Wide Web has many sites for individuals and businesses. Imagine that you are going to start your own desktop publishing business. Explore the Web and examine home pages for other companies. List the features you think should be included in your page and make a sketch of how your page might look.

To complete this independent challenge:

a. Start Publisher if necessary, then open a new blank full-page publication.

b. Decide what features you want your ideal home page to have, and list these features.

c. Connect to the Internet and use any search engine (such as Yahoo!) to find sites for desktop publishing companies.

d. Sketch a design for your company's home page.

e. Sketch a logo for your company.

f. Describe your findings.

g. Disconnect from the Internet.

h. Complete your publication. Be sure to include your name in the publication.

i. Print the publication, save, and exit Publisher.

▶ Visual Workshop

Open the publication PUB A-4 on your Project Disk and add the text shown in Figure A-20, using the skills you learned in this unit. The font size in the text frame is 16 point. Save the publication as Image Masters Gift Card on your Project Disk. Be sure to include your name in the Publication. Print the publication.

FIGURE A-20

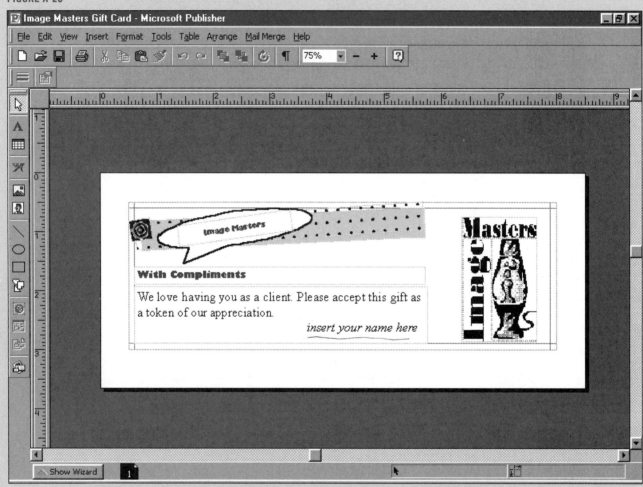

Publisher 2000

Unit B

Creating
a Publication

Objectives

- ► **Plan and design a publication**
- ► **Create a publication with the Catalog**
- ► **Replace frame text**
- ► **Add a graphic image**
- ► **Add a sidebar**
- ► **Add a pull quote**
- ► **Use the Design Gallery**
- ► **Group objects**

Now that you are familiar with the Publisher workspace and understand how to open and save a file, you are ready to create your own publication. You will learn how to use the Catalog to create a new publication, replace existing text, and add a graphic image to the publication. Marjorie Raynovich, an intern at Image Masters, is learning how to use Publisher. She is on the newsletter team and is working on the latest issue.

Planning and Designing a Publication

Before you start a publication, you have to plan and design it. Planning involves knowing what information to include and identifying who will be reading it. Knowing the content and your audience helps you decide how the publication should look. Marjorie's first assignment is to create a one-page newsletter. She wants the newsletter to catch the eye of her readers. She includes the company logo (which is in electronic form), to identify the newsletter as Image Masters', and calls attention to specific text she wants to be sure is seen and understood. Marjorie reviews the following planning guidelines.

Details

Determine the purpose of the publication

Publisher lets you create a wide variety of publications using the Catalog. The subject matter is critical in determining the style and layout. By answering a few simple questions, Marjorie can create the appropriate type of publications for any task.

Identify the readers

Knowing who will be reading your publication dictates your writing style and your presentation of the text. Since the company employees will read the Image Masters newsletter, it should be informative but retain a sense of humor. Marjorie also knows that clients sometimes read the newsletter, so she'll make sure that they are mentioned and that the newsletter always portrays Image Masters positively.

Prominently feature the company logo

The Image Masters logo appears on all its print material: letterhead, envelopes, business cards, and advertisements, to reinforce the identity of the company. Naturally, Marjorie wants to include the logo in the newsletter.

Replace placeholders with text

A publication created using the Catalog includes placeholder text frames in its page design. These **placeholders** contain text that can easily be replaced with text that you type directly in Publisher or with previously created Word documents. This simulated text lets you see how text looks on the page, without being distracted by its content. Marjorie can easily replace these placeholders with meaningful text.

Emphasize certain text

Some text on a page should stand out. Refer to Figure B-1. Marjorie will use a pull quote to pique the interest of readers. She'll use a sidebar to add emphasis to a particular article.

FIGURE B-1: Sample newsletter

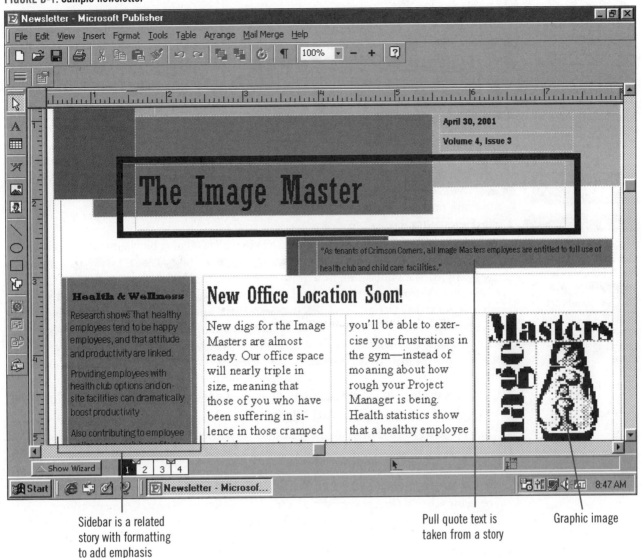

Sidebar is a related story with formatting to add emphasis

Pull quote text is taken from a story

Graphic image

Creating a Publication with the Catalog

The Catalog wizards make it easy to choose the type of publication you want. Tabs within the Catalog let you choose the type of publication you want, by type or design. After answering a few simple questions, a wizard creates all the necessary elements you need to get started quickly. Marjorie uses the Catalog Wizard to create a newsletter.

Steps

Trouble?

If Publisher is already open, open the Catalog dialog box by clicking File on the menu bar, then clicking New. If you don't see wizards displayed in the Catalog dialog box, see your instructor or technical support person.

1. **Start Publisher**

   The Microsoft Publisher Catalog dialog box opens. This dialog box helps you get started by letting you choose among: Publications by Wizard, Publications by Design, or Blank Publications. The Publication by Wizard tab is organized by the types of available publications (such as Brochures, Flyers, Business Forms, or Web Sites). The Publications by Design tab is organized by Design Sets (such as Master Sets, Holiday Sets, Restaurant Sets, or Special Paper), which are each then organized by design schemes (such as Arcs, Blocks, or Bubbles). The Blank Publications tab contains a variety of publications such as Web pages and cards that contain no formatting or objects. The default Wizard selection is Quick Publications, as shown in Figure B-2. You want to create a newsletter.

2. **Click Newsletters in the Wizards list, click the image of the Blends Newsletter in the Newsletters list, then click Start Wizard**

   The Newsletter Wizard displays the Introduction and explains that the wizard will help you customize the layout of your newsletter with a series of wizard screens in which you specify the features of your publication.

3. **Click Next, then click Crocus in the Color Scheme list**

   The color scheme Crocus provides an array of purples and golds. Compare your screen to Figure B-3. As you click each color scheme, the page sample changes to show you the effect on the newsletter.

4. **Click Next**

   The next series of wizard screens lets you choose the number of columns per page, whether a placeholder should be included for a customer address, how the newsletter should be printed, and which personal information set will be used.

5. **Click Next to accept the default value of three columns, click the Yes option button to insert the customer's address placeholder, click OK to accept the change to page 4, click Next, click Next to accept double-sided printing, click the Secondary Business option button, then click Update**

   The Personal Information dialog box opens. You have to verify that the Personal Information for the Secondary Business set is correct.

6. **If necessary, change the entries to Carlos Mendoza in the Name text box, Account Executive in the Job or position title text box, Image Masters, Crimson Corner, Suite 200, Santa Fe, NM, 87501 in the Address text box, Phone: 505-555-5555, Fax: 505-555-4444, Email carlos.mendoza@imagemasters.com in the Phone/fax/e-mail text box, Image Masters in the Organization name text box, We make you look your best in the Tag line or motto text box, click Update, then click Finish**

   The newsletter is displayed in the workspace, as shown in Figure B-4.

7. **Click the Save button 🖫 on the Standard toolbar, click the Save in list arrow, locate your Project Disk, type IM Newsletter in the File name text box, then click Save**

FIGURE B-2: Microsoft Publisher Catalog dialog box

Available wizards are displayed here

FIGURE B-3: First screen in Newsletter Wizard

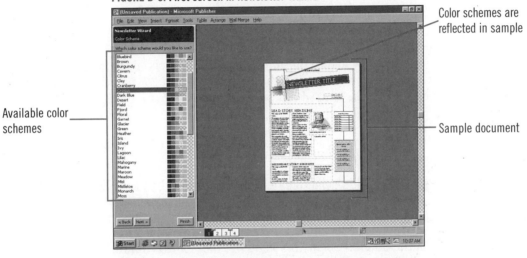

Color schemes are reflected in sample

Available color schemes

Sample document

FIGURE B-4: Completed newsletter

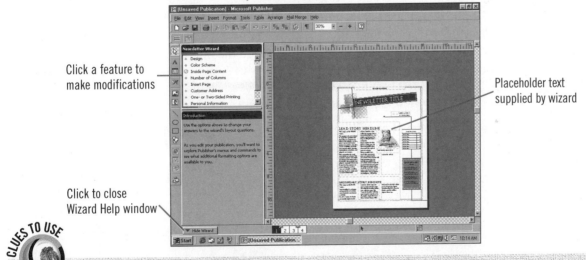

Click a feature to make modifications

Placeholder text supplied by wizard

Click to close Wizard Help window

CLUES TO USE

Types of Catalog publications

The Catalog is a visual directory containing more than 1600 different types of publications. Each selection offers a variety of choices within its particular category. Publications created using the Catalog can be easily modified using readily available wizards. If the wizard is not displayed, click the Show Wizard button ▲ Show Wizard , then click the feature you want to modify. Brochures, for example, are available in many different styles and layout schemes. Labels can be created for floppy disks, audiocassettes, and videocassettes, and CD case liners.

Replacing Frame Text

You can either type text directly into a frame or you can insert documents created in a word processor, such as Microsoft Word. Since the Catalog created placeholders for you, you can edit the existing text frames. Marjorie needs to replace the placeholders in the newsletter she created earlier with the text she has written. She inserts a Word document and types replacement text.

Steps

QuickTip

Hide the Office Assistant, if necessary.

1. Click the **Hide Wizard button** ▼ Hide Wizard

The wizard is no longer visible, although you can always redisplay it by clicking the Show Wizard button.

2. Click the **Lead Story Headline**, as shown in Figure B-5

Handles surround the selected text. The formatting toolbar appears below the Standard toolbar. A balloon with Help text may appear next to the selected text. This assistance is called a **tippage**. To turn tippages on or off, click Tools on the menu bar, click Options, click the User Assistance tab, click the Show tippages check box to deselect it, then click OK. Zooming into the selected text can help you get a closer look.

QuickTip

You can zoom by clicking the Select Zoom Mode button, which always displays the Zoom factor, or click the Zoom In and Zoom Out buttons.

3. Press **[F9]**

You may have to use the scroll bars to position the selected text. The text in this text frame is just a placeholder; you have to type the text for this heading.

4. Press **[Ctrl][A]** to select **Lead Story Headline**, then type **New Office Location Soon!**

The typed text replaces the text placeholder in all capital letters. The columns beneath the heading contain placeholder text provided by the wizard.

5. Click the **column** below this heading, then press **[Delete]**

Now that the text frame is empty, you insert an existing Word document into it.

Trouble?

If you receive an error message advising you that Publisher can't import the specified format because this feature is not currently installed, and asking if you would like to install it now, insert the Office 2000 Disc 2 CD, then follow the instructions to install the feature. If you need further assistance, ask your instructor or call a technical support person.

6. Click **Insert** on the menu bar, click **Text File**, locate the files on your Project Disk, click **PUB B-1**, then click **OK**

You might have to use the scroll buttons to see the new text. Compare your newsletter to Figure B-6. Instead of using the menu bar to insert text from a document file, you can right-click a text frame, point to Change Text, then click Text File.

If you want to view the full page of the newsletter, you can Zoom out so it fits the screen.

7. Press **[F9]**, then click the **Save button** 🖫 on the Standard toolbar

FIGURE B-5: Selected text frame

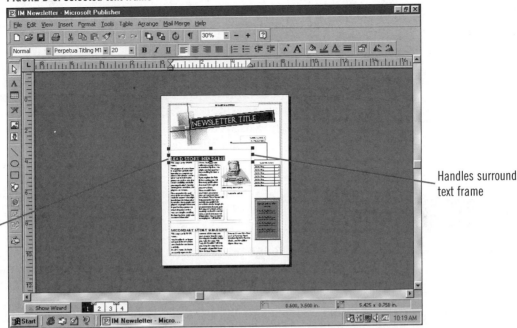

Lead story headline

Handles surround text frame

FIGURE B-6: Word document text in newsletter

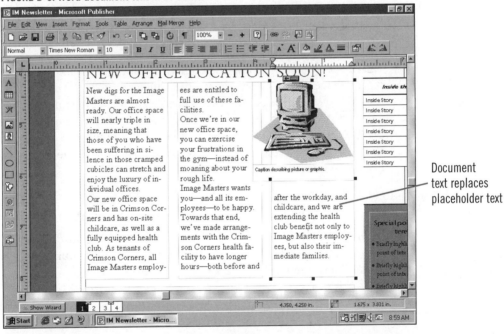

Document text replaces placeholder text

Resizing a frame

A frame—whether it contains text or a graphic image—can be resized. Once a frame is selected, you can change its size by placing the mouse pointer over a handle and then dragging it. The pointer may change to ⬚, ⬚, ⬚, or ⬚, depending on the handle you place the pointer on. If, for example, the ▣ ••• button appears at the end of a selected frame, it may be possible to resize the frame, enabling the text to fit. Figure B-7 shows a text frame being diagonally resized to make it shorter and narrower.

FIGURE B-7: Resizing a text frame

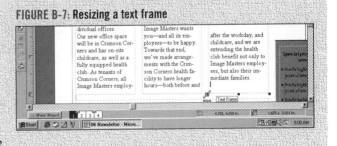

Adding a Graphic Image

Artwork in a publication can express a feeling that might take hundreds of words to accomplish. In electronic form, a piece of artwork is called a **graphic image**. **Clip art** is a collection of graphic images supplied on a disk. Publisher comes with thousands of pieces of clip art. Artwork can also be scanned into your computer, purchased separately, or created using drawing programs. Table B-1 lists some of the common graphic image formats that can be used in Publisher. Marjorie incorporates the logo—already in electronic form—into her newsletter. She begins by selecting the graphic image of a computer that is a placeholder, and zooming to better view the image.

Steps

1. Click the **graphic image placeholder**, then press **[F9]**

Handles surround the placeholder, indicating that it is selected. Next, you replace the placeholder artwork with the electronic logo file.

2. Click **Insert** on the menu bar, point to **Picture**, then click **From File**

The Insert Picture File dialog box opens. The default view is Preview, which shows you a sample of the selected image in the right side of the dialog box. It defaults to the My Pictures folder. You use the Im-logo file.

3. Click the **Look in list arrow**, locate your Project Disk, click **Im-logo**, as shown in Figure B-8, then click **Insert**

The Image Masters logo appears in place of the graphic placeholder. The wizard included a caption beneath the graphic image placeholder that can be changed later. An image can be resized by placing the pointer over a handle and then dragging the frame edge to specify the new size. As you drag the pointer, the status bar reflects the object's size and position, using the ruler coordinates. To preserve an image's scale while increasing or decreasing its size, you can press and hold the [Shift] key while dragging the frame's edge. You want the image to be in the same location, but larger.

QuickTip

Ruler coordinates in this book are given as follows: 3½" H/6½" V; this means 3½" on the horizontal ruler, 6½" on the vertical ruler.

4. Place the pointer over the lower-left handle of the image so it turns to ⌐, press and hold **[Shift]**, press the left mouse button, drag the ⌐ pointer to **3½" H/6½" V**, as shown in Figure B-9, release **[Shift]**, then release the mouse button

As you drag the frame, lines move on the rulers to guide your actions, and the outline of the image changes in size. You want to see the full-page image.

5. Press **[F9]**

Pleased with how the image looks, you save your work.

6. Click the **Save button** 🖫

FIGURE B-8: Insert Picture File dialog box

Available graphic images appear here

Preview of selected file

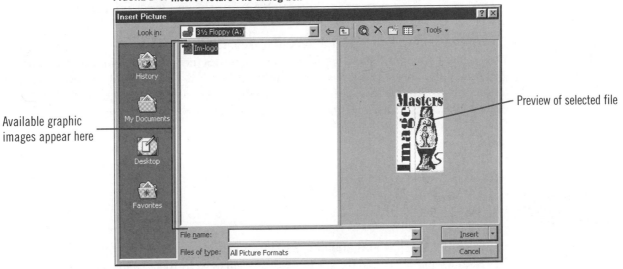

FIGURE B-9: Resizing a graphic image

3½" on the horizontal ruler

6½" on the vertical ruler

Outline of the image as it is being resized

Coordinates change as image is being resized

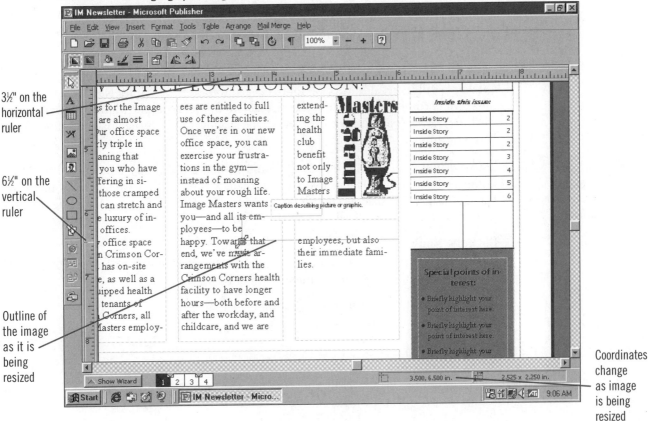

TABLE B-1: Common graphic image formats

graphic image	extension	graphic image	extension
Bitmap	.BMP	Tagged Image File Format	.TIF
PC Paintbrush	.PCX	JPEG Picture Format	.JPG or .JPEG
Graphics Interchange Format	.GIF	Windows Metafile	.WMF
Encapsulated PostScript	.EPS	CorelDraw	.CDR

Adding a Sidebar

Information not vital to a publication can make interesting reading when placed to the side of the regular text in a **sidebar**. A sidebar sometimes uses the same size font as regular body text, but it may also appear in a larger size or different font. Sidebars can be dramatized by adding a border or shading. ✏️ Marjorie replaces the sidebar placeholder with text in a Word document. She starts by selecting the placeholder and enlarging her work area.

Steps

1. **Click the sidebar placeholder, as shown in Figure B-10, then press [F9]**
   Handles appear around the sidebar, which is enlarged to 100%. While most of the body text in this newsletter is in the Times New Roman font, the Font button on the Formatting toolbar shows that the text in the sidebar placeholder is formatted in the Eras Demi ITC font. The Catalog created this style. By default, the sidebar text frame has a border, background fill, and formatting to make it stand out. Now you insert the sidebar text prepared in Word.

2. **Press [Ctrl][A] to select the text, click Insert on the menu bar, click Text File, click PUB B-2, then click OK**
   The new text appears in the text frame. Notice that the original formatting set up by the Catalog is still there, although the font changed to reflect the Times New Roman font of the Word document, and the font size changed to fit the text in the frame. You want to see what the sidebar looks like with a shadow. The shadow can be turned on and off using the Format menu.

QuickTip

If necessary, click the arrow at the bottom of the menu to view the additional commands.

3. **Click Format on the menu bar, click Shadow, then press [Esc] to deselect the frame**
   Compare your work to Figure B-11. A gray shadow is behind the white background containing the text. The shadow effect is not as evident in some styles, and you decide you prefer the way the sidebar looked without the shadow.

4. **Click the Undo button** 🔄 **on the Standard toolbar**
   It is a good idea to save your work early and often in the creation process, especially before making significant changes to the publication or before printing.

5. **Click the Save button** 💾 **on the Standard toolbar**
   You want to see the full-page image.

6. **Press [F9]**
   All the text fits nicely inside the frame.

FIGURE B-10: Sidebar placeholder selected

Text Frame tool

Handle

Text frame

Sidebar placeholder

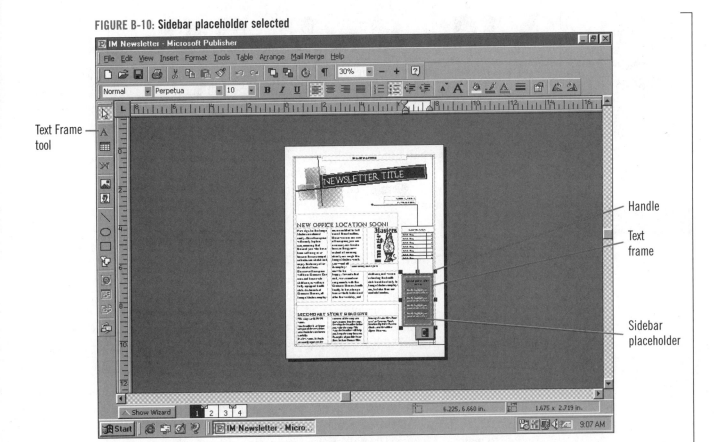

FIGURE B-11: Sidebar text inserted in publication

Current zoom level

Sidebar with shadow

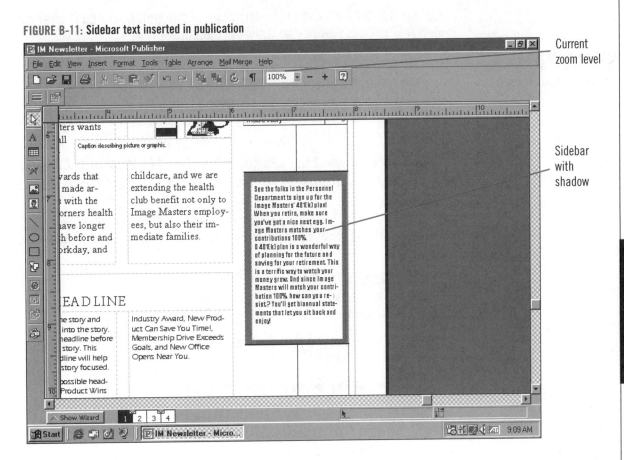

Adding a Pull Quote

To invite a reader to look at an article, a short statement, or pull quote, is often extracted from the text and set aside from the body of the text. Often the pull quote uses a different font and size from the body text. It does not have to be identical to text found in the body, but should be similar. A pull quote should be on the same page as the article from which it came, and in close proximity to it. It should also be long enough to be interesting, but short enough to be read quickly and easily. If a pull quote is not already in your publication, you can add one using the Design Gallery. The Design Gallery button—located on the Objects toolbar to the left of the workspace—guides you. ✏ Marjorie inserts a pull quote on the first page above the image for the article on new office space.

Steps 1 2 3 4

1. **Click the Design Gallery Object button ▣ on the Objects toolbar**
   The Design Gallery opens. The Design Gallery is organized into three tabs: Objects by Category, which lets you select the type of object to add to a publication; Objects by Design, which helps you organize your objects into a uniform design; and Your Objects, for special objects you can create and save. A fourth tab, Extra Content, will appear when you use a wizard to change from one Publisher-designed publication to another, and Publisher needs the Extra Content tab to store objects that don't fit or match the new design.

2. **Click the Objects by Category tab (if necessary), click Pull Quotes in the Categories list, click Blends Pull Quote, then click Insert Object**
   You select the Blends Pull Quote because you used the Blends Newsletter and you want the pull quote to match the design. The pull quote placeholder appears on the first page of the publication, as shown in Figure B-12. You can place the pull quote anywhere in the publication.

3. **Place the pointer over the upper-left edge of the pull quote so it changes to ⊕🚚, drag the left frame edge to ½" H/2¾" V, then press [F9]**

4. **Place the pointer over the bottom-right edge of the pull quote so it changes to ◱, then drag the frame edge to 3½" H/3½" V**
   Compare your pull quote to Figure B-13. The pull quote sits just above the New Office Location Soon! heading. When the pull quote is selected, the horizontal scale becomes active, just as with any text frame.

5. **Click at 1" H/3" V, select the pull quote text, type "As tenants of Crimson Corners, all Image Masters employees are entitled to full use of the health club, then press the SpaceBar**
   The remaining words you have to type look as if they will not fit in the frame. However, Publisher's **AutoFit feature** automatically resizes the font and forces the text to fit in the frame.

6. **Type and childcare facilities."**
   As you typed, Publisher made the text fit by changing the font size. Compare your pull quote to Figure B-14. You want to see the full-page image.

7. **Press [F9], then press [Esc] to deselect the pull quote**
   Now you save your work.

8. **Click the Save button 💾 on the Standard toolbar**

Trouble?

The AutoFit feature should be set to Shrink Text On Overflow by default to make the text fit the frame. Click Format on the menu bar, click AutoFit Text to check the settings.

FIGURE B-12: Pull quote added to publication

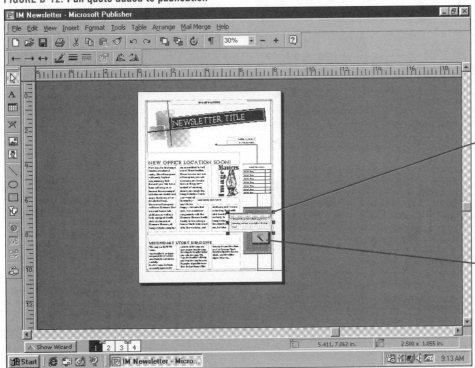

Pull quote placeholder may be in a different location

Click Wizard button to change formatting

FIGURE B-13: Moved and resized pull quote

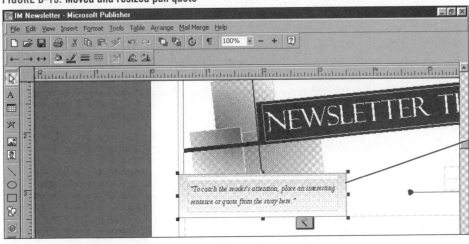

As it is resized, the pull quote's design is automatically modified

"To catch the reader's attention, place an interesting sentence or quote from the story here."

FIGURE B-14: Completed pull quote

Font is automatically scaled so text fits in pull quote

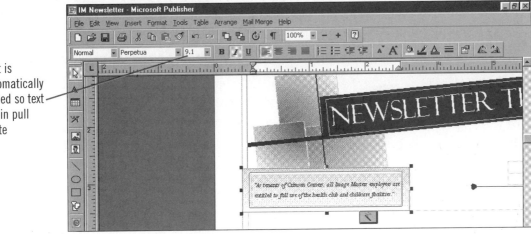

"As tenants of Crimson Corners, all Image Masters employees are entitled to full use of the health club and childcare facilities."

Using the Design Gallery

Publisher uses the Design Gallery to assemble a publication quickly. In addition to adding a pull quote, you can use the Design Gallery to easily insert a Publisher-designed object such as an ad, calendar, coupon, or logo. ▟▟▟▟ Marjorie uses the Design Gallery to create an advertisement in the right column of the newsletter. First, she resizes the existing text frame to make room on the page.

Steps

1. Click the **sidebar** at **7" H/7" V**, position the pointer over the sidebar, drag the pointer ⊥ to **6" V** to move the object up, press **[F9]**, then press **[Esc]** to deselect the frame
An advertisement will fit nicely beneath the moved text frame. Beneath the article, you insert an announcement advertising an Image Masters benefit sale.

2. Click the **Design Gallery button** 🖼 on the Objects toolbar, click **Advertisements** in the Categories list, scroll through the available predesigned advertisements and note the differences, click the **Equal Emphasis Advertisement box**, as shown in Figure B-15, then click **Insert Object**
The Advertisement object is inserted on the page, but it is not necessarily positioned correctly. You want the object beneath the resized text frame.

3. Place the pointer over the object and drag the 🚚 pointer so the bottom-right edge is at **8" H/10¼" V**

4. Place the pointer over the top-left handle and drag the 🔳 pointer so the top-left edge is at **6¼" H/8¾" V**
The ad is displayed as shown in Figure B-16. It is made up of several objects. As with all objects placed by Publisher, you have to edit the placeholder text.

5. Click **Advertisement Heading**, then type **Benefit Sale**
Although you don't currently have all information needed to complete the advertisement, you enter the remaining information that you do have.

6. Click the **text beneath Benefit Sale**, type **July 25, 2001**, click the **text beneath the date** and type **Call** *insert your name here*, click the **text above Benefit Sale**, type **Support Battered Family Victims.**, then press **[Esc]**
Your screen should look like Figure B-17. Once you are finished, you can zoom out and save your work.

7. Press **[F9]** to zoom out, then click the **Save button** 💾 on the Standard toolbar

FIGURE B-15: Advertisements category in the Design Gallery

Tabs organize
Catalog
subjects

Active
category

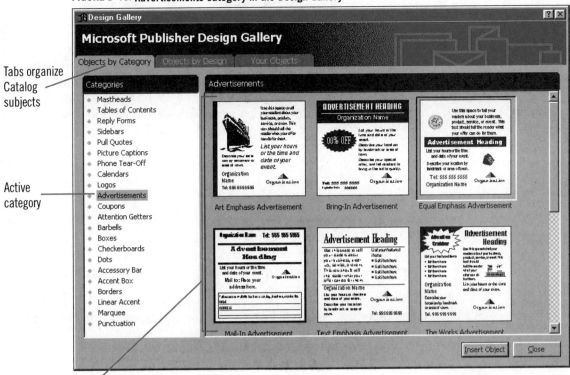

Available
Advertisements

FIGURE B-16: Ad created with the Design Gallery

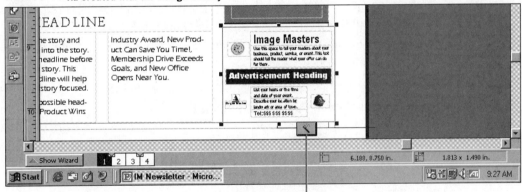

Click Wizard button
to change format

FIGURE B-17: Benefit Sale ad

Your name
identifies
this as your
publication

Grouping Objects

Once many objects are positioned on a page, you may find that you want to move one or more of them. Moving a single object is as simple as selecting it, then dragging it to a new location. But it gets more complicated when more than one object is involved and you want to retain relative positions. **Grouping**, or turning several objects into one object, is an easy way to move multiple items. Later, you can always **ungroup** them for individual modifications, turning the combined objects back into individual objects. Marjorie wants to reduce the width of the caption under the Image Masters logo. To change the size of the caption text frame, she needs to ungroup the objects, make her modifications, and then regroup the logo and caption.

Steps

1. Click the **Image Masters logo and caption** at **5" H/5" V**, press **[F9]**, then click the **Ungroup Objects button** ⊞ beneath the selected object

Instead of black handles surrounding one object, gray handles surround each selected object, as shown in Figure B-18. The Ungroup Objects button is now a Group Objects button.

2. Click the workspace to deselect the ungrouped objects, click the caption at **5" H/6¼" V**, select the **caption text**, then type **You'll be seeing our logo around Crimson Corners**

The new caption is beneath the logo.

3. Position the pointer over the **left-middle handle of the caption**, so that the ⟷ pointer appears, then drag the edge of the frame to **4⅜" H**

The new caption displays in the resized text frame. You notice that the logo splits the word "extending" in an awkward way. Moving the logo will correct the placement of text around the graphic image.

Trouble?

You may have to resize and move the logo to get all the text to appear below the logo.

4. Position the ⊕ pointer over the logo, press and hold **[Shift]**, drag the left edge of the logo to **4½" H**, then release **[Shift]**, as shown in Figure B-19

Since you ungrouped the objects to modify the caption and logo, you want to group them now that you are finished.

5. Make sure the caption is still selected, press and hold **[Shift]**, click anywhere within the logo, then click the **Group Objects button** ⊡

Compare your newsletter to Figure B-20. You decide to save your work and print the first page of the newsletter.

6. Press **[F9]**, then click the **Save button** 🖫 on the Standard toolbar

7. Click **File** on the menu bar, click **Print**, click the **Current page option button**, then click **OK**

A copy of the publication is printed. You end your Publisher session.

QuickTip

Look for your name in the advertisement to distinguish your work from a classmate's.

8. Click **File** on the menu bar, then click **Exit**

FIGURE B-18: Preparing to group objects

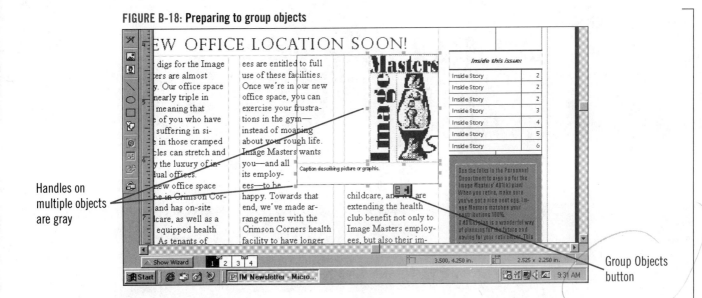

Handles on multiple objects are gray

Group Objects button

FIGURE B-19: Resized caption

FIGURE B-20: Regrouped logo and caption

Single set of handles surrounds grouped object

Practice

► Concepts Review

Label each of the elements of the Publisher window shown in Figure B-21.

FIGURE B-21

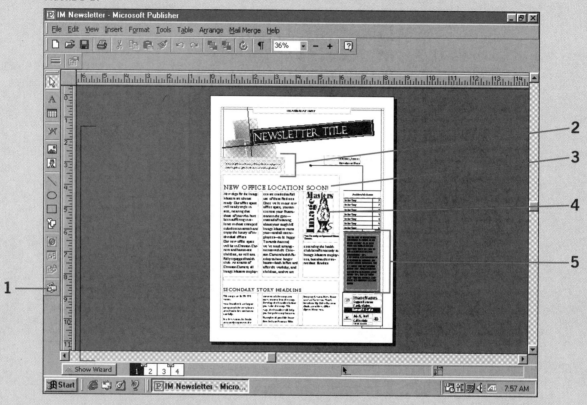

Match each of the terms or buttons with the statement that describes its function.

6. [A]
7. ⬚ RESIZE
8. **Catalog**
9. **Tippage**
10. 🖼
11. **Graphic image**

a. Creates an ad or logo
b. Assistance that appears on the screen
c. Resizes a frame
d. Creates a text frame
e. Artwork stored in an electronic file
f. Helps create a publication

Select the best answer from the list of choices.

12. Turn off an individual tippage by pressing
    a. [Ctrl]
    b. [Alt]
    c. [Shift]
    d. [Esc]

13. Maintain scale while resizing a graphic image by pressing
    a. [Esc].
    b. [Alt].
    c. [Shift].
    d. The right mouse button.

14. Which of the following extensions does not indicate a common graphic image format?
    a. .GIF
    b. .TIF
    c. .CDR
    d. .GFX

15. Interesting information that invites you to read a story is called a
    a. Placeholder.
    b. Sidebar.
    c. Pull quote.
    d. Heading.

16. Which of the following statements about a pull quote is false?
    a. It should be on a different page from the actual text.
    b. It should be short and easy to read.
    c. It does not have to be identical to the text in the article.
    d. It should entice you to read the article.

17. Which of the following statements about graphic images is false?
    a. Scanned artwork can be used in Publisher.
    b. Artwork created in drawing programs can be used in Publisher.
    c. You can use only the artwork that comes with Publisher.
    d. You can use any electronic artwork in Publisher.

18. Which button is the Design Gallery button?
    a.
    b.
    c.
    d.

19. Which pointer is used to change the location of an object?
    a.
    b.
    c.
    d.

20. Group objects by holding and pressing [Shift], clicking each object, then clicking
    a.
    b. Tools on the menu bar, then Group Objects.
    c.
    d. Objects on the menu bar, then Group.

► Skills Review

1. **Create a publication with the Catalog.**
   a. Start Publisher.
   b. Using the Catalog, select the Newsletter Wizard on the Publications by Wizard tab.
   c. Work your way through the wizard: Select the Floating Oval Newsletter, with the Monarch color scheme, two columns, no placeholder for the customer's address, double-sided printing, and the Personal Information set for the Secondary Business.
   d. Save this publication as Mock-up Newsletter on your Project Disk.

2. **Replace frame text.**
   a. Hide the Wizard.
   b. Select the Lead Story Headline placeholder.
   c. Zoom in using the [F9] key.
   d. Replace the placeholder text with the following: "Office Space Design Hints."
   e. Select the lead story text, then delete it.
   f. Insert the file PUB B-3.
   g. View and read the article.
   h. Save the publication.

3. **Add a graphic image.**
   a. Select the graphic image placeholder. Click the Ungroup button.
   b. Right-click the image, point to Change Picture, point to Picture, then click From File. Insert the picture file Im-logo from your Project Disk.
   c. Zoom out so you can see the entire publication.
   d. Save the publication.

4. **Add a sidebar.**
   a. Select the sidebar placeholder in the left column (above the table of contents).
   b. Zoom in to view the Special Points of Interest placeholder text in the sidebar.
   c. Delete all the placeholder text.
   d. Insert the Word file PUB B-4.
   e. View and read the sidebar.
   f. Zoom out so you can see the entire publication.
   g. Deselect the sidebar.
   h. Save the publication.

5. Add a pull quote.

a. Click the Design Gallery button on the Objects toolbar, click Pull Quotes, then add a pull quote, using the Floating Oval style.

b. Zoom in to view the pull quote.

c. Move the pull quote so the upper-left edge is at 2½" H/2½" V.

d. Replace the existing placeholder text with the following: "There are some tricks of the trade that go beyond spending a lot of money."

e. Resize the pull quote frame so the lower-right edge is at 6" H/2¾" V. It should be placed above the Office Space Design Hints text frame.

f. Zoom out so you can see the entire publication.

g. Deselect the pull quote.

h. Save the publication.

6. Use the Design Gallery.

a. Click the Design Gallery button.

b. Create an attention getter using the Brick Attention Getter.

c. Zoom in to view the object.

d. Reposition the object so the top-left edge is at 5¼" H/7½" V.

e. Position the pointer over the lower-right handle, then resize the object to 7" H, using [Shift] to preserve the image's scale.

f. Replace the text "Free Offer" with "*Insert your name here's* Logo Designs."

g. Deselect the attention getter object.

h. Zoom out so you can see the entire publication.

i. Save the publication.

7. Group objects.

a. Use Zoom and [Shift] to select both the volume and newsletter date text frames (in the left column).

b. Group the two selected objects.

c. Move the grouped object so the top of the volume text frame is at 2½" V.

d. Ungroup the objects.

e. Deselect the objects.

f. Save your work.

g. Print the first page of the publication.

h. Exit Publisher.

▶ Independent Challenges

1. Your local Kiwanis Club has hired you to design a flyer for its upcoming fund-raiser: a Fun Walk. The organization is trying to raise money for a local homeless shelter. The funds will go toward materials, food, clothing, maintenance, and refreshments for volunteers.

To complete this independent challenge:

a. Start Publisher if necessary.

b. Create a flyer using the Catalog.

c. Use the Charity Bazaar Fund-raiser Flyer.

d. Make up the information necessary, such as the location of the fund-raiser, the address of the Kiwanis Club, and the date and time of the event.

e. Change the Color Scheme to floral, and accept the default options for Customer Address.

f. Modify the "Charity Bazaar" text placeholder to say Kiwanis Fun Walk.

g. Replace the five bulleted items with five of your own good reasons to attend this event.

h. Include your name as the contact person for the event.

i. Make sure all the text in the flyer relates to the Fun Walk event.

j. Save the publication on your Project Disk as Fun Walk flyer.

k. Print the publication.

l. Close the publication.

2. You've decided to create a menu for the take-out division of the Get It While It's Hot luncheonette. Use the Catalog to create this menu. Replace the existing text with your own.

To complete this independent challenge:

a. Start Publisher if necessary.

b. Use the Catalog to create a take-out menu.

c. Choose the Scallops Take-Out Menu.

d. Change the Color Scheme to Berry, and accept the default options for Customer Address.

e. Modify the placeholder company name and information for the Get It While It's Hot luncheonette.

f. Replace the five bulleted items with five of your own good reasons to purchase from this luncheonette.

g. Include your name as the contact person for take-out orders.

h. Make sure all the text in the flyer relates to the take-out menu.

i. Make up your own menu items. (*Hint:* Click the Page 2 icon to access the second page.)

j. Group two objects on the menu and move them.

k. Modify the existing coupon to 15%.

l. Save the publication on your Project Disk as Take-Out Menu.

m. Print the publication.

3. The tenants in your rental property have just given you 30 days notice, so you need to find new tenants. You can easily create a sign in which you can describe the house.

To complete this independent challenge:

a. Start Publisher if necessary.

b. Use the Catalog to create a Sign using the For Rent Sign.

c. Modify the telephone number placeholder using your own number.

d. Replace the bulleted items with your own descriptions of the house for rent.

e. Create a text frame above the telephone number that says "Call *insert your name here* for more information."

f. Select the text containing your name, then make the font size 18 points.

g. Save the publication on your Project Disk as For Rent Sign.

h. Print the publication.

i. Close the publication.

4. You've been asked to create a Web page for your school's Publisher class, using the Catalog. This site should discuss what topics are covered in the class.

To complete this independent challenge:

a. Log on to the Internet and use your browser to go to your school's Web site.

b. Print out the home page and the page for the department offering this Publisher course.

c. Start Publisher if necessary.

d. Use the Catalog to create a Web site for your Publisher class.

e. The Web page should consist of one page, using the style, color scheme, and background that complements the school's existing design scheme.

f. Create a text frame that lists you as the contact person if more information is necessary. Adding a telephone number, fax number, or e-mail address is optional.

g. Replace the text placeholders with your own text, based on the topics that are covered in this class. (*Hint:* Consult your class syllabus.)

h. Save your publication as Publisher Class Web Page on your Project Disk.

i. Be sure to include your name on the Web page.

j. Print your publication.

k. Close the publication.

▶ **Visual Workshop**

Use the Catalog to create an informational postcard for Image Masters that announces its new location. Use the Borders Informational Postcard layout, use the quarter page format, and show only the address on the other side of the card. Print one postcard in the center of the page, for your secondary business. Add the Im-logo graphic image, apply the Garnet color scheme, and replace the placeholder text, using Figure B-22 as a guide. If you need to identify your printout, add a text frame to the publication with your name. Save the publication as IM Postcard on your Project Disk.

FIGURE B-22

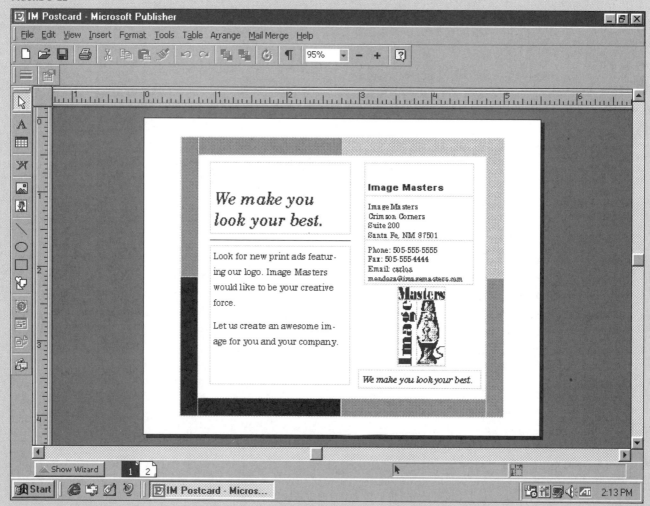

Unit C

Formatting

Text

Objectives

► **Use layout guides**
► **Use ruler guides**
► **Format a frame**
► **Add bullets and numbering**
► **Check spelling**
► **Modify a smart object**
► **Paint formats**
► **Add a table**

You've learned some of the basics about creating a publication: using the Catalog, adding a graphic image, and replacing placeholders with text. Now you'll learn how to use more powerful tools available in Publisher. These tools help you design and lay out text and graphics to create publications that look consistent and professional. ✒️ Emily Martin is an editorial assistant for Image Masters. She is designing a flyer that will be used to promote Image Masters' Professional Design Clinic. Emily uses many Publisher tools to create the flyer.

Using Layout Guides

If correctly laid out, each publication has specific elements placed to achieve an exact and consistent look. This consistency occurs only with careful planning. **Layout guides**, horizontal and vertical lines visible only on the screen, help you accurately position objects within a page and across pages in a publication. ◄ Emily's assignment is to design a flyer for an upcoming design clinic. She uses a publication from the Catalog and then sets up the layout guides.

Steps

1. Start Publisher

The Microsoft Publisher Catalog opens with the Publications by Wizards tab selected.

2. Click Flyers in the Wizards list, click Informational, click Bars Informational Flyer in the Information Flyers list, then click Start Wizard

The flyer appears on the screen. Simple modifications can be made using the Wizard.

3. Click Personal Information, click the Secondary Business option button, click Update, then, if necessary, change the entries to Carlos Mendoza in the Name text box, Account Executive in the Job or position title text box, Image Masters, Crimson Corner, Suite 200, Santa Fe, NM, 87501 in the Address text box, Phone: 505-555-5555, Fax: 505-555-4444, Email carlos.mendoza@imagemasters.com in the Phone/fax/e-mail text box, Image Masters in the Organization name text box, We make you look your best in the Tag line or motto text box, then click Update

4. Click the Save button 🖫 on the Standard toolbar, click the Save in list arrow in the Save as dialog box, locate your Project Disk, type Design Clinic Flyer in the File name text box, then click Save

The Wizard makes it easy to make adjustments to your publication, such as changing the color scheme.

5. Click Color Scheme in the Flyer Wizard, click Cranberry in the Color Scheme list box, then click Hide Wizard

The image and text frames inserted by the Wizard are not necessary for the flyer you are designing.

6. Right-click the image at 5" H/5" V, click Delete Object, click Yes in the warning box, right-click the text frame at 5" H/8" V, then click Delete Object

The image and text frames are deleted from the flyer.

7. Click Arrange on the menu bar, then click Layout Guides

The Layout Guides dialog box opens, as shown in Figure C-1. Layout guides create a grid that helps you line up elements such as images and text frames on the page.

8. Click the Columns up arrow until 3 appears in the text box, click the Rows up arrow until 3 appears in the text box, as shown in Figure C-2, then click OK

The pink lines represent the column guides, while the blue lines represent the column guide margins. The guides appear on the screen, as seen in Figure C-3, but do not print on the page.

9. Click the Save button 🖫 on the Standard toolbar

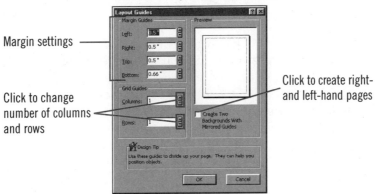

FIGURE C-1: **Layout Guides dialog box**

Margin settings

Click to change
number of columns
and rows

Click to create right-
and left-hand pages

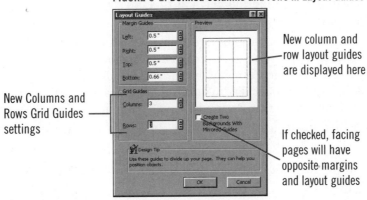

FIGURE C-2: **Defined columns and rows in Layout Guides dialog box**

New column and
row layout guides
are displayed here

New Columns and
Rows Grid Guides
settings

If checked, facing
pages will have
opposite margins
and layout guides

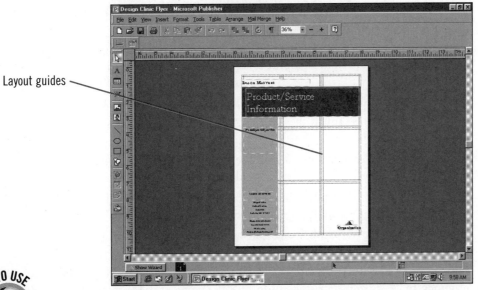

FIGURE C-3: **Layout guides in publication**

Layout guides

Modifying layout guides

Layout guides can only be adjusted from the background view. If a publication has left and right pages, you can use **mirrored guides**, so that facing pages will have opposite margins and layout guides. Switch to the background view by clicking View on the menu bar, then clicking Go to Background. When you press [Shift] and place your pointer over a layout guide, the pointer changes to either a vertical or a horizontal adjust pointer. Drag the guide to any location, using the vertical and horizontal rulers for exact measurements. You can also return layout guides to their original location by clicking the Undo button 🔄 on the Standard toolbar. To return to the foreground view, click View on the menu bar, then click Go to Foreground.

Using Ruler Guides

In addition to the power of layout guides, Publisher lets you create individual page guides. **Ruler guides** work just like layout guides but are created in the foreground of individual pages. Functionally, layout guides and ruler guides are the same. (Layout guides are on the background of *each* page in a publication; ruler guides are in the foreground on individual pages.) Visually, ruler guides are green horizontal and vertical lines that are dragged from the rulers into the workspace. The location of zero, the **zero point**, on both the vertical and horizontal rulers can be moved, giving you the flexibility to make precise measurements from any point on the page.

Emily moves each ruler's zero point and adds ruler guides for the location of a graphic image on the first page. First, she moves the vertical ruler closer to the page.

Steps

1. **Click the vertical ruler, when the pointer changes to ⟷, press and hold the left mouse button, drag the vertical ruler to the left edge of the publication, as shown in Figure C-4, then release the left mouse button**
   When you move a ruler, the zero point does not change, the ruler just moves closer, making it easier to locate positions. You don't need to move the horizontal ruler since it sits just above the top of the page. Currently, the horizontal and vertical zero point is set at the top-left edge of the page. You would like to move the horizontal and vertical zero point to the left edge and top margin so you can determine exact measurements from the top-left margin edge.

2. **Position the mouse over the Move Both Rulers button at the intersection of the horizontal and vertical rulers, press and hold [Shift], right-click the Move Both Rulers button, drag the ✛ pointer to ½" H/½" V, release the mouse button, then release [Shift]**
   Compare your rulers and zero points to those shown in Figure C-5.

3. **Place the ⇖ at the top-left corner of the pink guides**
   The coordinates in the Object position are displayed as 0.000, 0.000 in. Having the zero points at the top-left margin helps you position the rulers so you can make accurate measurements. To further help you line up elements, you can add ruler guides, sometimes called **ruler guide lines**. You want a graphic image to appear 3" from the left margin and 3½" from the top margin.

4. **Press and hold [Shift], position the pointer anywhere over the vertical ruler, drag the ⇔ pointer to the 3" mark on the horizontal ruler, release [Shift], then release the mouse button**
   A green vertical ruler guide appears on the screen at the 3" horizontal mark. Use the same techniques to create a horizontal ruler guide, using the horizontal adjust pointer.

5. **Press and hold [Shift], position the pointer over the horizontal ruler, drag the ⇕ pointer to the 3½" mark on the vertical ruler, release [Shift], then release the mouse button**
   After looking at the horizontal ruler guide, you realize its position is too high and that the ruler guide needs to be lowered.

6. **Press and hold [Shift], position the pointer over the horizontal ruler guide until it changes to ⇕, drag the ruler guide to 3¾" on the vertical ruler, then release [Shift]**
   The ruler guides—which do not print—appear only on this page and will be helpful when a text frame is added.

7. **Place the pointer on the vertical ruler, press and hold [Shift], drag the ⇔ pointer to create one vertical ruler guide at 5½"**

8. **Place the pointer on the horizontal ruler, press and hold [Shift], drag the ⇕ pointer to create three horizontal ruler guides: one at 6¼", one at 7", and one at 8¾"**
   Compare your ruler guides to those in Figure C-6.

9. **Click the Save button 🖫 on the Standard toolbar**

FIGURE C-4: Moving a ruler

Move Both Rulers button

Current zero point

New location of vertical ruler

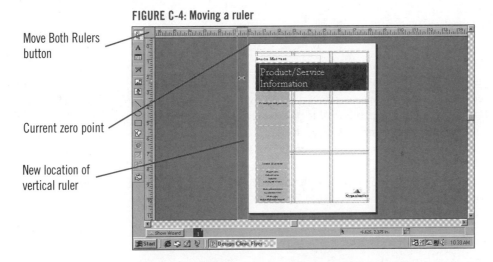

FIGURE C-5: Vertical ruler and zero points moved

New zero point

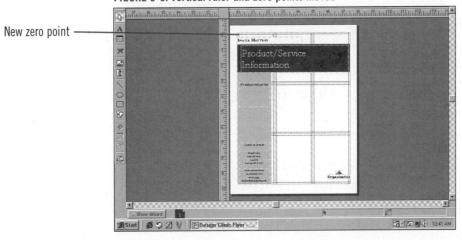

FIGURE C-6: Horizontal and vertical ruler guides added

Horizontal ruler guide

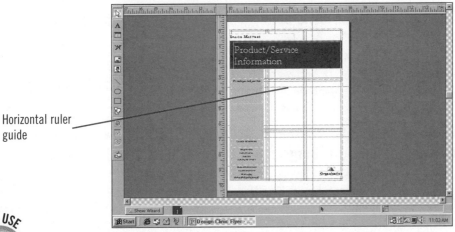

Using Snap To commands

Publisher's Snap To commands let you take advantage of the layout and ruler guides. Turning on Snap To commands—Snap to Ruler Marks, Snap to Guides, and Snap to Objects—gives these guides a magnet-like effect, pulling whatever you're trying to line up toward the guide. Each of the Snap To commands is located on the Tools menu. Once the Snap To command is turned on, select the frame or object, move the pointer over the object until it changes to [MOVE], then drag the object's edge toward the new location until the object snaps in place.

Formatting a Frame

Ruler guides help place objects accurately on a page. Objects can snap to the guides or be placed "freely" on the page. Once a frame is added to a page, it can be moved or resized. A border can be added and formatted to appear in any available color or line width you choose. The **Formatting toolbar**, which is visible only when text or an object is selected, contains buttons for the most common commands used for improving the object's appearance. The buttons that appear on the Formatting toolbar depend on the type of object selected. ✒️ Emily wants to add a text frame that describes how to best use logos for clients. She places the frame using the ruler guides, and then enhances it with formatting attributes. To begin, she moves the vertical ruler out of the way.

Steps

1. Click the **vertical ruler**, when the pointer changes to ←→, drag the **vertical ruler** to the left edge of the workspace

2. Click the flyer heading at **2" H/2" V**, then type **Professional Design Clinic**
   Using the Ruler and Layout guides to place frames is extremely helpful, particularly when you use the Snap To feature.

3. Click **Tools** on the menu bar, verify that **Snap to Ruler Marks** and **Snap to Guides** have check marks next to the command names; if necessary, click **Snap to Ruler Marks** and **Snap to Guides** to select them

4. Click the **Text Frame Tool button** 🅰 on the Objects toolbar
   The pointer changes to ┼. The ruler guides help you easily place the text frame.

5. Drag the ┼ pointer from **3" H/3¾" V to 5"H/6¼" V**
   Did you notice that the frame snapped to the ruler and layout guides? Compare your page to Figure C-7.
   A thicker, more colorful border would make the frame stand out.

6. Click the **Line/Border Style button** ≡ on the Formatting toolbar, then click **More Styles**
   To create a black border, you could have selected one of the choices in the Line/Border Style button's list palette. Since you want to change the color and thickness of the border, you clicked More Styles to open the Border Style dialog box shown in Figure C-8. You could also change a border by clicking Format on the menu bar, then clicking Line/Border Style.

7. Click **4 pt line border thickness**, click the **Color list arrow**, click the **second box from the left Accent 1 (Burgundy)** in the Scheme colors palette, then click **OK**
   Since you selected a color scheme in the Wizard, these colors are presented to you on this palette to help you retain design consistency in the publication. You could click More Colors if you wanted to work outside the suggested colors. The text frame that you placed on the first page using the ruler guides is displayed with the thicker, burgundy border that matches the fill in the flyer heading, as shown in Figure C-9.

8. Click the **Save button** 💾 on the Standard toolbar

FIGURE C-7: Creating a text frame within ruler and layout guides

Text Frame Tool
button

Text frame

Line/Border Style
button

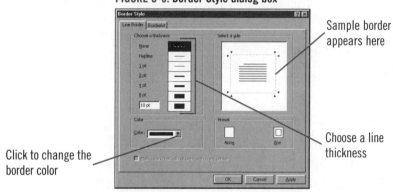

FIGURE C-8: Border Style dialog box

Sample border
appears here

Choose a line
thickness

Click to change the
border color

FIGURE C-9: Frame with thick, burgundy border

Border color
matches the fill in
the flyer heading

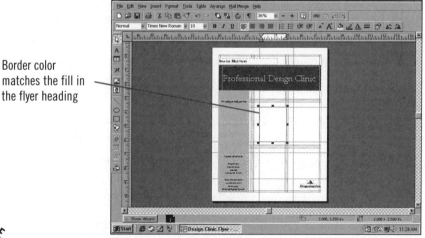

CLUES TO USE

Using different types of margins

When you think of margins, you probably think of the white space surrounding the four edges of a page. However, margins may be used to create white space anywhere on the page for clarity. Without them, the page would look cluttered and be hard to read. Margins occur around a graphic image, around each side of a column, and within a table or text frame. Any frame on a page has adjustable margins that can be changed by right-clicking the object, clicking Change Frame, then selecting the Text (or Object) Frame Properties—usually the next to the last command in the menu.

Adding Bullets and Numbering

Using paragraphs is an effective method of telling a story. When you need to display information in list form within a document, you can add emphasis to each item in the list by formatting the items with bullets or numbers. A **numbered list** is generally used to present items that occur in a particular sequence, while items in a **bulleted list** can occur in any order. Both numbered and bulleted list formatting can be applied either before or after the text has been typed. A numbered list can be created from the Formatting toolbar using the Numbering button; a bulleted list can be created using the Bullets button. You can switch back and forth between numbers and bullets—trying different styles of numbers and bullets—until you arrive at the right format. Emily enlarges the view of the area containing the new text frame, then types a sample numbered list in the text box she's just created.

Steps

1. **Make sure the text frame with the burgundy border is still selected, then press [F9]**
   You zoom in on the text frame. The point size for a list can be larger than that in a paragraph because you have less text and want to emphasize each word. Headings help identify content in list.

2. **Click the Font Size list arrow** 12 **on the Formatting toolbar, click 16, type Why use a logo?, then press [Enter]**
   The heading, which is not part of the numbered list, is entered first.

3. **Click the Numbering button** ▤ **on the Formatting toolbar, 1. appears in the text box, type It identifies your firm easily., press [Enter], type Customers start to look for it., press [Enter], then type It is a marketing tool; your firm's symbol.**
   Compare your text with Figure C-10. To apply numbers or bullets to *existing text*, you first must select the text you want to format, then click the Bullets or Numbering buttons to apply the formatting. To change from numbers to bullets, you only need to select a <u>few</u> words or place the insertion point in a line, then click ▤ to change to numbers or click ▤ to change to bullets

4. **Drag the I pointer to select the numbered text from It identifies to the word symbol so that the last three sentences are selected, then click the Bullets button** ▤ **on the Formatting toolbar**
   To enhance any list, you can change the appearance of the bullets. Publisher lets you use a variety of characters as the bullet as well as change the size (measured in points) of the bullet.

5. **Click Format on the menu bar, then click Indents and Lists**
   The Indents and Lists dialog box opens, as shown in Figure C-11. You can change the appearance of bullets by selecting a new bullet type.

QuickTip

Dragging all the text within a line (including the final hard return) reorganizes items in a numbered list.

6. **Click the diamond bullet (third from the left), then click OK**
   Compare your work with Figure C-12. You zoom out to see the full page.

7. **Click [F9]**
   The bullet list fits nicely on the page.

8. **Click the Save button** 🖫 **on the Standard toolbar**

FIGURE C-10: Numbered list in a text frame

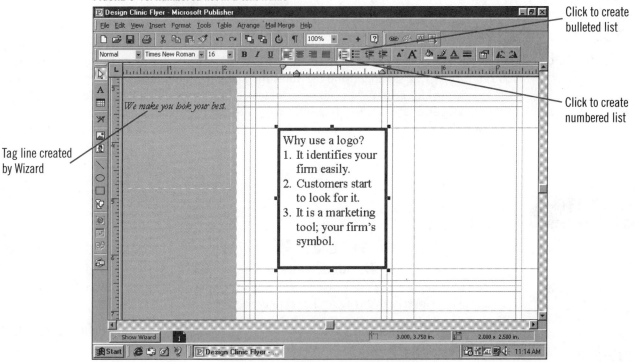

Tag line created by Wizard

Click to create bulleted list

Click to create numbered list

FIGURE C-11: Indents and Lists dialog box

Click to change the type of list

Click to change the bullet type

Sample list is displayed here

FIGURE C-12: Numbered list changed to a bulleted list

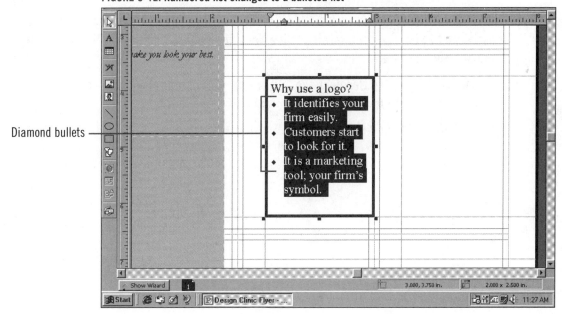

Diamond bullets

Publisher 2000

Publisher 2000

Checking Spelling

Spelling errors can ruin the most beautifully designed and well-written publication. Fortunately, using Publisher's spelling checker means you won't have to be embarrassed by misspelled words. You can easily check spelling using the Tools menu, or by right-clicking a text frame. Spelling errors are shown immediately as you type, indicated by a wavy red underline. You can add correctly spelled personal or industry-specific words not already in the Publisher dictionary, as you work. ▰▰▰ Emily adds a text frame and then imports text into the publication. Once the text is inserted, she checks for spelling errors.

Steps

1. Click the **Text Frame Tool button** [A] on the Objects toolbar, drag the + pointer from 5½" H/3¾" V to 7⅜" H/6¼" V (using Snap To features), then press **[F9]**

The text frame appears on the page. Text in a text frame is sometimes referred to as a **story**. You want to insert a prewritten story into the text frame.

2. Click **Insert** on the menu bar, click **Text File**, click **Pub C-1** on your Project Disk, then click **OK**

The text stored in the document file Pub C-1 is inserted into the text frame as shown in Figure C-13. This text contains misspelled words (identified on the screen by wavy red underlines) that you can correct.

> **Trouble?**
>
> The Check Spelling option on the Tools menu—as well as the Check Spelling command within Proofing Tools (when you right-click)—is available only if a text frame is selected. Check the spelling of an individual word by clicking anywhere within the word before pressing [F7].

3. Click **Tools** on the menu bar, point to **Spelling**, then click **Check Spelling**

The Check Spelling dialog box opens, as shown in Figure C-14. The first incorrect word found is "shpeaker." Often, Publisher correctly guesses a word's spelling and places it in the Change to text box, so you don't have to click a suggestion. You can simply replace the incorrect word with the word already in the Change to text box.

4. Click **Change**

The spelling checker advances to the next misspelled word, stopping at "ytears." This word is incorrect and should be "years."

5. Click **Change**

Publisher continues correcting all spelling errors in this text frame.

> **QuickTip**
>
> To choose not to accept Publisher's suggestion, click Ignore.

6. Click **event** in the suggestions list, click **Change** to correct **ewent** to **event**, correct **seshions**, correct **tipbs**, correct **Captaine**, click **No** in the warning dialog box, then click **OK**

Compare your corrected text to Figure C-15.

7. Click the work space to deselect the text frame, then press **[F9]**

The corrected story in the text frame is next to the bulleted list.

8. Click the **Save button** [💾] on the Standard toolbar

FIGURE C-13: Spelling errors in text

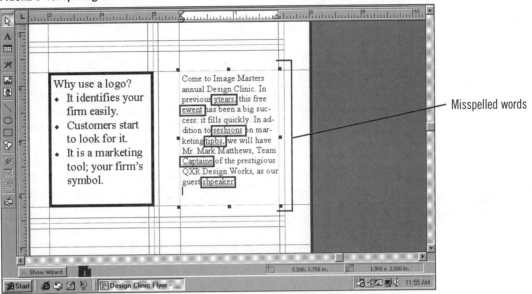

Misspelled words

FIGURE C-14: Check Spelling dialog box

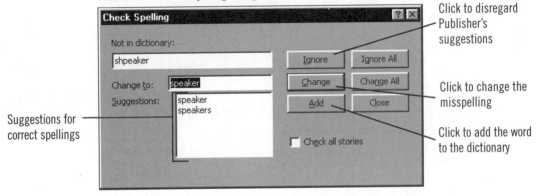

Click to disregard
Publisher's
suggestions

Click to change the
misspelling

Click to add the word
to the dictionary

Suggestions for
correct spellings

FIGURE C-15: Text after spelling has been checked and corrected

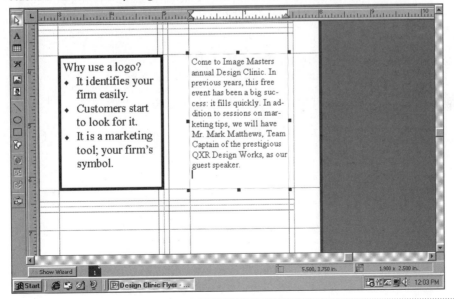

Modifying a Smart Object

When you use the Catalog to create a publication, you may find objects within that publication that contain a wizard button. These smart objects contain text or graphic images from a Personal Information Set. They make it easy to keep publication information consistent. Many Design Gallery elements contain smart objects. This feature offers an easy way to change the content of a publication while ensuring accuracy. Design Sets also help to create a consistent style for elements in the publications. Emily wants to add the logo to the publication's smart object and then add an Attention Getter from the Design Gallery.

Steps 1234

1. **Click the smart object at 7" H/9" V, press [F9], then click the Wizard button** beneath the object
   The Logo Creation Wizard is displayed, as shown in Figure C-16.

2. **Click the Picture file that I already have option button, then click Insert Picture.**
   The Insert Picture dialog box opens, defaulting to the My Pictures folder.

> **Trouble?**
>
> If the logo was already added to the Personal Information Set, close the Logo Creation Wizard and skip to Step 5.

3. **Click the Look in list arrow, locate the lm-logo file on your Project Disk, then click Insert**
   A message box appears, informing you that you have modified the logo in this Publication. It asks if you want to save the new logo in the Secondary Business Personal Information Set.

4. **Click Yes in the message box, then click the Logo Creation Wizard close box**

5. **Click the workspace, Press [F9], click the Design Gallery Object button on the Objects toolbar, click Attention Getters in the Categories list, click the Arrowhead Attention Getter, then click Insert Object**
   The ruler guides help you position the new object.

6. **Place the pointer on the Attention Getter object, use to drag the Attention Getter to 5¾" H/3¼" V (using the Snap To feature), then press [F9]**
   Compare your work to Figure C-17.

7. **Position the pointer over the lower-middle handle, then drag the pointer up to 3¾" V, click Free Offer in object's text frame, then type Special Guest**
   Notice how the AutoFit feature resized the text to fit within the object, as shown in Figure C-18.

8. **Click the work space, then press [F9]**
   The Design Clinic Flyer is looking very professional.

> **Trouble?**
>
> If necessary, click Yes to save the logo to the Personal Information set.

9. **Click the Save button on the Standard toolbar**

FIGURE C-16: Logo Creation Wizard

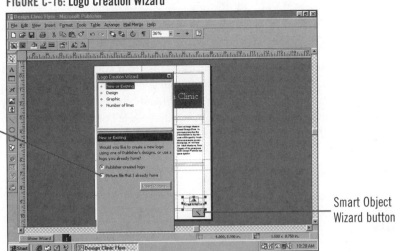

Click to insert an existing graphic image

Smart Object Wizard button

FIGURE C-17: Smart object positioned on page

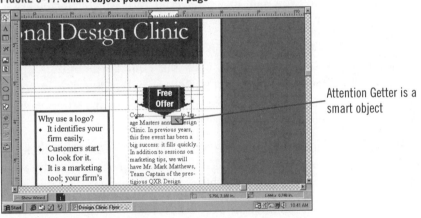

Attention Getter is a smart object

FIGURE C-18: Resized smart object

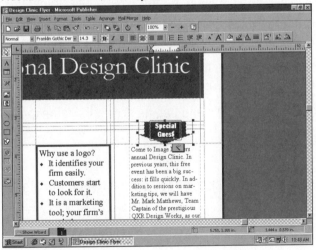

CLUES TO USE

Using a Design Set

The Design Gallery contains many **Design Sets**— elements in the gallery that share common themes, colors, or objects. You can also create your own design set by first selecting an object, clicking the Your Objects tab, clicking the Options button, then clicking Add Selection To Design Gallery. The Add Object dialog box opens, allowing you to name the object.

Painting Formats

Toolbar buttons can be used to apply object formatting or text attributes such as bold, italics, increased or decreased font sizes, or different colors. To apply the attribute to existing text, select the characters, then click the appropriate button on the Formatting toolbar. This process can get repetitive, especially if more than one attribute is applied to characters. To help you apply formats easily and consistently, you can use the Format Painter button on the Standard toolbar, or you can select the text and use the Format menu to pick up the formatting, and then apply the formatting. ✎ Once Emily applies formats to text, she uses the commands available to apply the same formatting to other text.

Steps

1. Click anywhere within the **text frame** with the burgundy border, then press **[F9]**
The text frame is zoomed in on the screen. To draw attention to certain words in each sentence, you want to apply specific formats. One method of formatting is to use buttons on the Formatting toolbar.

2. Drag the ⌶ pointer over **logo** in the first sentence, click the **Bold button** **B** on the Formatting toolbar, click the **Font Color button** **A**, click **More Colors**, click the **Basic colors option button**, click the **Blue box in column 1**, then click **OK**
You also want this text to be in small capital letters and have a shadow. Attributes can be applied using the Font dialog box.

3. Click **Format** on the menu bar, click **Font**, then click the **Small caps check box**
Compare your Font dialog box to Figure C-19. You can add as many attributes as you want by clicking the check boxes in this dialog box.

4. Click the **Shadow check box**, then click **OK**
Now that the formatting attributes have been applied, you can paint them on other text.

5. Click the **Format Painter button** 🖌 on the Standard toolbar, note that the pointer changes to 🖌⌶, place the pointer in the text box, then drag the 🖌⌶ pointer over **identifies**
You can also pick up and apply formats using the Format menu.

6. Click **Format** on the menu bar, click **Pick Up Formatting**, then double-click **look**
You can use the Format menu to apply the formatting you just picked up.

7. Click **Format** on the menu bar, as shown in Figure C-21, then click **Apply Formatting**

8. Click 🖌, then select **marketing tool**
Now all your formatting is complete.

9. Press **[F9]**, then click the **Save button** 🖫 on the Standard toolbar

FIGURE C-19: Font dialog box

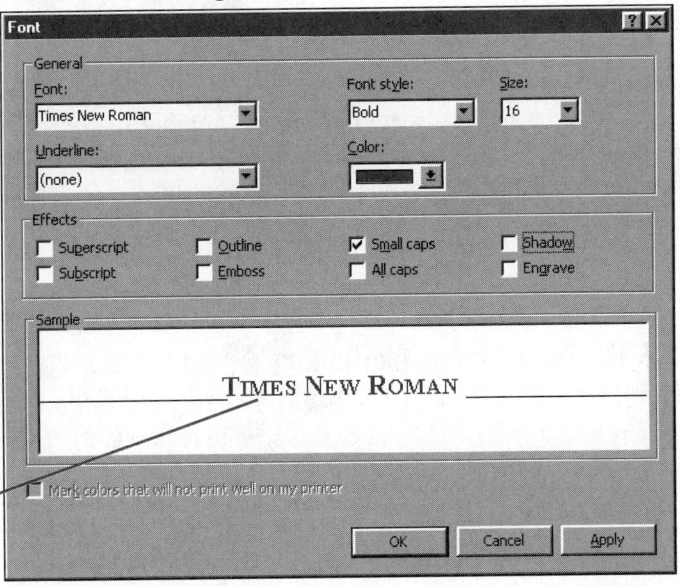

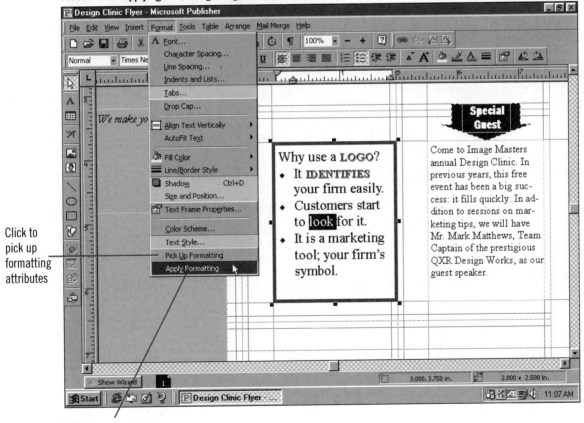

Sample of current formatting

FIGURE C-20: Applying formatting using the Format menu

Click to pick up formatting attributes

Click to apply picked-up attributes

Adding a Table

Some information is more easily understood if it is contained in a table. A table is created by first drawing a table frame, then determining the number of columns and rows that are needed. There are 23 table formats from which you can choose. Emily wants to include a table that contains a preliminary agenda for the design clinic.

Steps

1. **Click the Table Frame Tool button 🖽 on the Objects toolbar, then drag the ＋ pointer from 3" H/7" V to 7½" H/8¾" V** *(using the Snap To feature)*

   The Create Table dialog box opens, as seen in Figure C-21. The available table formats contain combinations of formatting, borders, and shading. Regardless of the table format you choose, you are free to change the numbers of columns and rows to fit your needs.

2. **Scroll down, click List with Title 2 in the Table format list, double-click the Number of columns text box, type 3, then click OK**

   The table appears in the table frame. You can type directly in the cells of the table, pressing [Tab] to move from cell to cell. The column headings are entered in the first row.

3. **Press [F9], type Session Title, press [Tab], type Description, press [Tab], then type Speaker**

   When first created, table cells are all the same width. Your second column will contain the most information, so you want to widen that column and make column 3 narrower. When you place the pointer between column selector buttons, it changes to the Adjuster pointer. Dragging the column with this pointer will change the size of the table. You change the width of a column but retain the same size of the table by holding [Shift], then dragging the Adjuster to the new width. You move a column by placing the pointer on the column selector buttons and, when the pointer changes to the Mover, dragging the column to a new location.

4. **Place the pointer in the column heading between the Description and Speaker columns until the pointer changes to ⬄, press and hold [Shift], the ScreenTip will display Adjust Width of Selected columns without changing table size, drag the ⬄ pointer to 6½" H, release the mouse button, then release [Shift]**

   You can now enter information in the table.

5. **Enter the table data using Figure C-22 as a guide**

6. **Replace Martin with your own last name, click outside the table to deselect it, then press [F9] to zoom out**

   You are pleased with the progress of the flyer and want to print it. You save, print, and exit Publisher.

7. **Click the Save button 🖫 on the Standard toolbar, click the Print button 🖨, then exit Publisher**

FIGURE C-21: Create Table dialog box

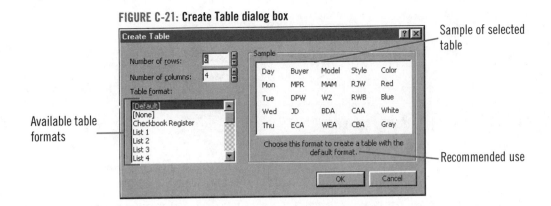

Available table formats

Sample of selected table

Recommended use

FIGURE C-22: Completed table

Column selector buttons

Session Title	Description	Speaker
Marketing Mayhem	Tips and tricks	Matthews
Logo Larceny	What constitutes theft?	Bunin
Hi-Tech Blues	Professional results on a budget	Duffy
Co-op Advertising	Getting more and paying less	Pinard
Spreading the Word	Reinforcing your image	Martin

Row selector buttons

CLUES TO USE

Using Auto Format

An existing table's design can be changed using the Auto Format feature. The Auto Format feature looks similar to the Create Table dialog box, except that it contains only table formats. Open the Auto Format dialog box, shown in Figure C-23, by clicking Table on the menu bar, then clicking Table Auto Format. Choose a Table Format, then click OK. You can change the number of columns and rows even after a table is created by using the Insert Rows Or Columns command on the Table menu or by right-clicking the mouse from within the table and selecting Change Table.

FIGURE C-23: Auto Format dialog box

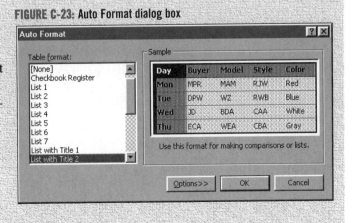

Practice

► Concepts Review

Label each of the elements of the Publisher window shown in Figure C-25.

FIGURE C-24

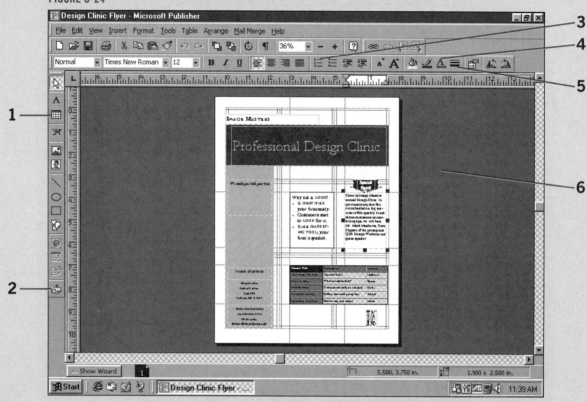

Match each of the buttons with the statement that describes its function.

7. ADJUST
8.
9.
10.
11.
12. B

a. Changes font color
b. Smart Object Wizard
c. Paints formatting attributes
d. Moves text
e. Makes text bold
f. Changes a column's width

Select the best answer from the list of choices.

13. Resize a column in a table while holding
   a. [Shift]
   b. [Alt]
   c. [Ctrl]
   d. [Esc]

14. Draw a table frame when the pointer turns to
    a.
    b.
    c. $+$
    d.

15. Ruler guides are
    a. Blue
    b. Green
    c. Pink
    d. Red

16. Each of the following is true about layout guides, *except*
    a. Objects can snap to them.
    b. They occur on every page in a publication.
    c. They appear in the background.
    d. They appear in the foreground.

17. Which of the following is not a font attribute?
    a. Bold
    b. Design
    c. Italics
    d. Shadow

18. Each of the following buttons is used for formatting, *except*
    a.
    b.
    c.
    d.

19. Modify a smart object by
    a. Double-clicking any element within it.
    b. Using a command on the Edit menu.
    c. Clicking the Wizard button on the Standard toolbar.
    d. Clicking the Smart Object Wizard button.

20. The Spell Checker in Publisher
    a. Identifies misspelled words.
    b. Finds all spelling and grammatical errors.
    c. Gets rid of the red wavy lines.
    d. Starts automatically.

▶ Skills Review

1. **Use layout guides.**
   a. Start Publisher.
   b. Use the Catalog's Flyers Wizard, select the Event design with the Bluebird color scheme, and create a flyer for a company picnic, then save the file on your Project Disk as Company Picnic flyer.
   c. Add layout guides.
   d. Use the Layout Guides dialog box to create three columns and three rows in this publication.
   e. Save your work.

2. **Use ruler guides.**
   a. Move the vertical ruler closer to the page so that you can better view the workspace.
   b. Adjust the zero points of the horizontal and vertical rulers to the top-left edge of the page margins.
   c. Create horizontal ruler guides at ¼", 1", 7½", and 9".
   d. Create vertical ruler guides at ½", 4", 5¾" and 7".
   e. Save your work.

3. **Format a frame.**
   a. Move the vertical ruler back to its original position.
   b. Click the text frame at 1" H/5" V.
   c. Zoom in to view the text frame.
   d. Create a four pt Accent 1 (blue) border around the text frame.
   e. Zoom out so you can see the full page.
   f. Deselect the text frame.
   g. Save your work.

4. **Add bullets and numbering.**
   a. Select the text frame at 5" H/5" V.
   b. Zoom in to the text frame.
   c. Replace the text with the following information:
      Volleyball,
      Dunk the boss,
      Sack race,
      Softball,
      Pie-eating contest.
   d. Change the bullet style to a 12 pt open arrowhead. (*Hint*: Use the Size up and down arrow boxes to change the bullet size.)
   e. Zoom out, then save the publication.

5. **Check spelling.**
   a. Select and zoom in to the text frame at 1" H/5" V.
   b. Replace the existing text in the frame with the text file PUB C-2 from your Project Disk.
   c. Check the spelling of the selected text.
   d. You should find four spelling errors.
   e. Do not check the spelling in the rest of the publication.

f. Zoom out so that you can see the entire publication.

g. Deselect the highlighted text.

h. Zoom out and save the publication.

6. Modify a smart object.

a. Click the Design Gallery button on the Objects toolbar.

b. Click the Attention Getters category.

c. Insert the Chevron Attention Getter.

d. Move and resize the object so it occupies the area from 5¾" H/¼" V to 7" H/1" V.

e. Zoom in to the object.

f. Change the text to "Too Much Fun!"

g. Click the Wizard button on the smart object.

h. Change the design to Hollowed Starburst.

i. Zoom out once you've viewed it.

j. Save the publication.

7. Paint formats.

a. Select and zoom in to the bulleted list.

b. Select the text Volleyball.

c. Format this text using the Engrave attribute and Accent 3 (Orange) color from the Scheme Colors.

d. Use the Format Painter to paint "Dunk the boss" with the same formatting.

e. Click the Format menu, then click Pick Up Formatting.

f. Use the Format menu to apply the formatting to the following text: Sack race, Softball, and Pie-eating contest.

g. Zoom out so that you can see the entire page.

h. Save your work.

8. Add a table.

a. Resize the two text frames (above the Contact person text frame) so their right edges end at 4" H. Delete the WordArt border element between the two frames.

b. Create a table frame from 4" H/7½" V to 7" H/9" V.

c. Use the List 3 format.

d. Create three columns and six rows. (Click Yes to create a table larger than the selected area.)

e. The column headings should be Activity, Contact, and Extension.

f. Enter the information in Table C-1.

g. Resize the columns so the left edge of the Extension column begins at 6¾" H.

h. Replace Greta Tolkmann's name with your own name.

i. Zoom out so that you can see the full page.

j. Deselect the table.

k. Save your work.

l. Print the publication.

m. Exit Publisher.

TABLE C-1

Activity	Contact	Extension
Volleyball	Lucy Evans	4328
Dunk the boss	Frank Etherton	4689
Sack race	Roger Hubbard	5220
Softball	Gail Farnsworth	1096
Pie-eating contest	Greta Tolkmann	3117

► ## Independent Challenges

1. The law firm of Eisner, Biheller, and Harpur has hired you to design a postcard that tells its clients about a promotion within the firm.

To complete this independent challenge:

a. Start Publisher if necessary, use the Invitation Cards Ascent Event Catalog Wizard to create an invitation that announces your promotion to partner, then save it as My Promotion Invitation on your Project Disk.

b. Use the Invitation Wizard to change the Suggested Verse.

c. Move the zero points to the top-left margin.

d. Add ruler guides to the second page so you'll know where to include new information. Ruler guides should create an area for a graphic image, such as a logo or photo, as well as an area for the new address.

e. Modify the Event Title (on page 2) to Promotion of Your Name, then modify the text beneath the Event Title to give details on your promotion as well as on the party.

f. On page 3, insert an element of your choice from the Design Gallery.

g. Modify any existing text to create a meaningful event invitation.

h. Create text that has bold and italic formatting.

i. Use the Format Painter to copy formats for the text.

j. Use the Spelling Checker to correct any errors in the text.

k. Save and print the publication.

l. Exit Publisher.

2. The seminar you are teaching in Business Leadership is about to end. At the conclusion, you would like to present each attendee with a certificate of completion.

To complete this independent challenge:

a. Start Publisher if necessary, use the (Plain Paper) Award Certificates Catalog Wizard to create a Certificate of Excellence Award Certificate.

b. Save the publication as Leadership Seminar Certificate on your Project Disk.

c. Move the zero points to the top-left margin.

d. Replace the Name of Recipient with your own name.

e. Format the Excellence Award text frame border so it is 4 pt, violet solid line.

f. Format the Name of Recipient text using the formatting of your choice.

g. Use the Spelling Checker to correct any errors in the text.

h. Save and print the publication.

i. Exit Publisher.

3. The local music appreciation society has asked you to design a program for their upcoming festival. To complete this independent challenge:

a. Start Publisher if necessary, use the Programs Catalog Wizard to create a Music Program, then save it as Music Program on your Project Disk.

b. On page 2, delete the existing table (for The Singers) and replace it with a three-column, eight-row table with the format of your choice.

c. Make up the names of the singers, the songs they will sing, and the type of music (for example, opera, folk, or jazz).

d. Enter your name on page 4 under Special Thanks.

e. Replace any existing text with information that creates a meaningful music program.

f. Format text using at least two attributes.

g. Use the Pick up and Apply Formatting commands to copy the formatting to other text.

h. Create a numbered list on the page for the events program.

i. Use the Spelling Checker to correct any errors in the text.

j. Save and print the publication.

k. Exit Publisher.

4. You've been hired to create a Web page for the KLIC radio station. This radio station is about to change its format and wants to use its Web site to promote the new format. KLIC also wants to use the Web site to announce a listener contest. Although you don't have all the details, you have enough to begin working on the site.

To complete this independent challenge:

a. Log on to the Internet.

b. While connected to the Internet, search your favorite browser for radio stations in your area. Research the types of contests other stations offer and the layout they use.

c. Use the Web Sites Catalog Wizard to create any style of one-page Web page, then save it on your Project Disk as KLIC Web Page.

d. Create a heading with the client's name.

e. Add a text frame that contains a bulleted list of the contest prizes.

f. Add a text frame that discusses the contest. Include your name and title: Contest Manager.

g. Format the text within the frame as necessary.

h. Add a colorful border to the frame.

i. Add an object from the Design Gallery to add emphasis to the page.

j. Use the Smart Objects Wizards button to change the object to a new design.

k. Replace any existing text with information that creates a meaningful Web page.

l. Use the Spelling Checker to correct any errors in the text.

m. Save and print the publication.

n. Exit Publisher.

▶ Visual Workshop

Use the Catalog to create an Estate Sale Flyer (use the Sale category in the Flyers Wizard). Save this publication on your Project Disk as Estate Sale Flyer. Use Figure C-25 as a guide. Replace all text as shown in the figure and change the bullets to diamonds. Include your name on the flyer. Save and print the flyer.

FIGURE C-25

Publisher 2000

Working

with Art

Objectives

- ► **Insert and resize clip art**
- ► **Copy and move an object**
- ► **Crop an image**
- ► **Align and group images**
- ► **Layer objects**
- ► **Rotate art**
- ► **Use drawing tools**
- ► **Fill drawn shapes**

Unlike novels, publications are not lengthy documents that require a lot of reading. Artwork enhances the understanding of a publication by complementing the text. Proper positioning of graphic images can relieve the monotony of text, add emphasis to the written word, and separate subjects. ◤ Mary Garrott, a graphics intern at Image Masters, is working on the artwork for a flyer for a hospital fund-raiser. Her responsibility is to lay out the artwork; the text will be added later.

Inserting and Resizing Clip Art

Publisher's extensive clip art collection makes it easy to dress up any publication. There is so much clip art available in the **Clip Gallery** that you can always find an image to represent a topic or round out a theme. You can use the Search feature to locate specific artwork by keyword or topic. The Clip Gallery contains pictures, motion clips, and sounds and is not limited to the artwork that comes with Publisher. You can personalize your installation—any electronic image can become a part of the Clip Gallery. Mary is ready to search for artwork for the flyer. After she adds it, she can resize it.

Steps

1. Start Publisher, click **Flyers** in the Wizards list, click **Fund-raiser**, click **Top Notches Fund-raiser Flyer**, click **Start Wizard**, then click **Finish** (if necessary)
   The flyer appears on the screen. Simple modifications can be made using the Wizard.

2. Click **Personal Information** in the Flyer Wizard, click the **Secondary Business** option button, click **Update**, then, if necessary, change the entries to **Carlos Mendoza** in the Name text box, **Account Executive** in the title text box, **Image Masters, Crimson Corners, Suite 200, Santa Fe, NM, 87501** in the Address text box, **Phone: 505-555-5555, Fax: 505-555-4444, Email** *carlos.mendoza@imagemasters.com* in the Phone/fax/e-mail text box, **Image Masters** in the Organization name text box, **We make you look your best** in the Tag line text box, then click **Update**

3. Click **Color Scheme** in the Flyer Wizard, click **Bluebird** in the Color Scheme list, click the **Save button** 🖫 on the Standard toolbar, locate your Project Disk, type **Fund-raiser Flyer** in the File name text box, then click **Save**
   A text frame can be resized to make room for artwork.

QuickTip

Ruler coordinates in this book are given as follows: 5" H/6" V; this means that 5" on the horizontal ruler 6" on the vertical ruler.

4. Click ▼ **Hide Wizard**, click the text frame at **5" H/5" V**, place the pointer over the **bottom-center handle**, drag the ⬍ pointer to 5" V, then press [Esc]
   The text frame is shortened and the text is deselected. The Clip Gallery contains the artwork you can use in the flyer.

5. Click the **Clip Gallery Tool button** 🔲 on the Objects toolbar, then drag the + pointer from **3" H/5" V to 4" H/6" V**
   You created a 1" × 1" frame, and the Insert Clip Art dialog box opens. The Clip Gallery contains tabs that organize Pictures, Sounds, and Motion Clips arranged by content. You want to find a picture of a hospital setting.

6. Click the **Search for clips text box**, type **hospital**, then press [Enter]
   The results of the search are displayed, as shown in Figure D-1. As you type, the AutoFill feature displays the word, as a ScreenTip. Press Tab at any time to accept the word displayed in the ScreenTip.

Trouble?

If you do not have the images used in this unit, choose similar ones from the Clip Gallery.

7. Right-click the **second image in the first row**, click **Clip Properties**, verify **HM00005_** in the Clip Properties dialog box, click **OK**, right-click the **second image in the first row**, click **Insert**, then click the **Close button** on the Insert Clip Art dialog box

8. Press [F9], place the pointer over the **bottom-right corner frame handle** until the pointer changes to ⬔, press and hold [Shift], drag the ⬔ pointer to 4¼" H/6¼" V, release the mouse button, then release [Shift]
   Compare the resized picture to Figure D-2.

9. Click the **Save button** 🖫 on the Standard toolbar

FIGURE D-1: Insert Clip Art dialog box after search

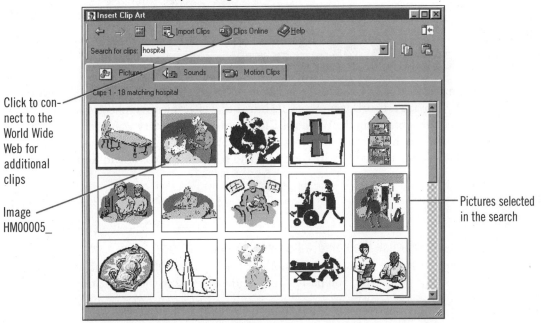

Click to connect to the World Wide Web for additional clips

Image HM00005_

Pictures selected in the search

FIGURE D-2: Clip art picture inserted and resized

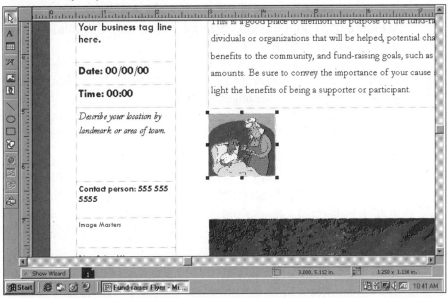

CLUES TO USE

Browsing the ClipGallery Live

Having access to the Internet means you can easily add to the Clip Gallery using the Microsoft ClipGallery Live Web site. This site offers a constantly changing selection of artwork. Figure D-3 shows some of the choices offered at this Web site. This site lets you constantly update your clip art so you always have new, exciting types of artwork to include in your publications. You can download clip art, photographs, sounds, and video clips from this Web site.

FIGURE D-3: Microsoft Clip Gallery Live Web site

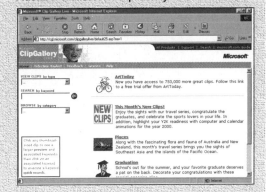

Copying and Moving an Object

Images can be inserted into a publication, then copied and moved to get just the right results. By copying artwork, you can create interesting effects with duplicated images. A copied image is held temporarily in the Windows **Clipboard**. Mary wants to copy a Clip Gallery image and move the copy to a new location. An object can be copied using several methods. You copy the selected object by right-clicking it and selecting the command from the pop-up menu.

Steps

QuickTip

You can also copy a selected object by clicking the Copy button 🖼 on the Standard toolbar, then paste it by clicking the Paste button 🖼.

1. Right-click the selected object, then click Copy

Although it looks as though nothing has happened, the clip art object has been copied to the Clipboard. Next, you paste a copy of the object into the publication.

2. Right-click the selected object, then click Paste

A copy of the object appears overlapping the original object, as shown in Figure D-4. The newly copied image is selected. You can now move the object within the publication.

QuickTip

Once it's on the Clipboard, you can repeatedly paste an object using any pasting method.

3. Click the horizontal scroll bar so you can see 8" H, position the pointer over the selected copy until it changes to 🚚, then drag the selected object so the upper-right corner is at 8" H/5" V

You can also copy a selected object quickly without copying to the Clipboard by dragging and dropping. **Drag and drop** by placing the pointer on the object, while you press and hold [Ctrl], drag the copy of the object using the quick copy pointer 🖰 to the new location, then release [Ctrl]. If you release [Ctrl] before you release the mouse and place the object, you will move the original instead of copying the object. Holding [Shift] while you move an object moves it in a straight line.

4. Position the pointer over the selected object until it changes to 🚚, press and hold [Ctrl], press and hold [Shift], then drag the 🖰 pointer so the left edge of the copy is at 5" H, release the mouse button, release [Shift], then release [Ctrl]

The second copy of the image is placed in a direct line to the right of the original object. You now have three images below the text box. You can easily delete any selected object.

5. Press [Delete]

The second copy is no longer displayed. You can flip an image to create mirror images and creative displays. This feature means you can create a mirrored image. A **mirrored image** has been flipped so that what was on the left side is now on the right side, as though you were viewing the object in a mirror.

6. Click the image at 7" H/6" V, then click the Flip Horizontal button 🔃 on the Formatting toolbar

The copy is flipped, as shown in Figure D-5.

7. Click the Save button 💾 on the Standard toolbar

FIGURE D-4: Pasted object overlapping original object

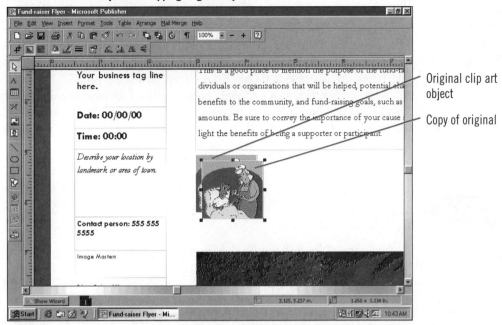

Original clip art object

Copy of original

FIGURE D-5: Flipped image

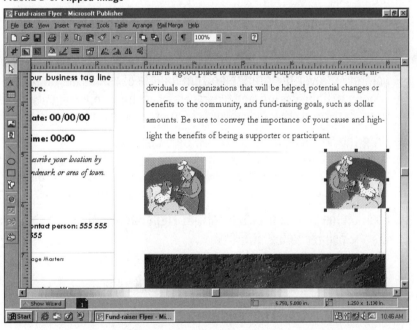

Using the Measurements toolbar

The Measurements toolbar lets you more precisely move, resize, or adjust graphic images or text. It can be displayed by clicking View on the menu bar, pointing to Toolbars, and then clicking Measurements. Figure D-6 shows the Measurements toolbar while a text frame is selected. (The available options in this toolbar depend on the type of object that is selected.)

This toolbar lets you make precise adjustments in an object's height, width, length, and rotation. Text point size, distance between characters, and line spacing can be adjusted using this toolbar.

FIGURE D-6: Measurements toolbar

| x 3 " | 5 " | 0.0 | 100 % | 0 pt |
| y 3.25 " | 1.75 " | | 100 % | 1.5 sp |

Cropping an Image

Even though Publisher comes with thousands of images from which to choose, you may find that the art you've chosen needs some modification. Perhaps parts of a picture's contents are not to your liking. In that case, you can always trim, or **crop**, portions of the artwork. A graphic image can be cropped vertically or horizontally—or both at the same time. Even though they are not visible, the cropped portions of an image are still there—they are just concealed. Mary will add an image from the Clip Gallery and crop unwanted portions of the image.

Steps 1 2 3 4

1. Click the **Clip Gallery Tool button** 📇 on the Objects toolbar, then drag the + pointer from **4¾" H/5" V to 6" H/6" V**
   The Insert Clip Art dialog box opens.

2. Click the **Search for clips text box**, type **anxiety**, then press **[Enter]**
   One image is displayed in the Clips 1-1 matching anxiety list.

3. Right-click the **image**, click **Insert**, then click the **Close button** on the Insert Clip Art dialog box
   Compare your page to Figure D-7. You want to crop the bottom of the image so that the man is concealed.

4. Click the **Crop Picture button** 🔳 on the Formatting toolbar, then place the Cropping pointer ✛ over the **center-bottom handle** of the anxiety image
   Cropping eliminates unwanted parts of images from appearing in a frame. A cropped image conceals parts of the whole image. You only want the image to show the file folder.

5. Drag the ✛ pointer up to **5½" H**, then click 🔳
   Look at the image as you trim it, to be sure the correct parts are cropped. The Crop Picture button stays selected until you click it to turn it off, so you can continue cropping until you are finished. Once the image is cropped, you can resize it to scale.

6. Position the pointer over the **bottom-right handle** so that it changes to ⬛, then drag the ⬛ pointer to **6¼" H/5¾" V**
   Compare your image to Figure D-8.

7. Click the **Save button** 💾 on the Standard toolbar

FIGURE D-7: Image before cropping

Crop Picture button

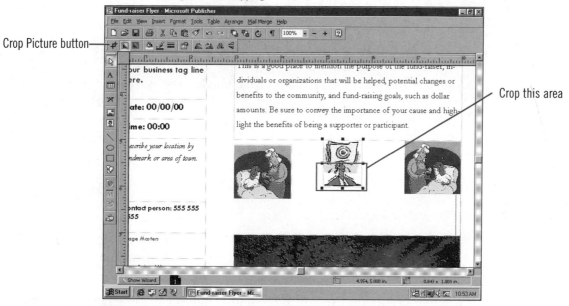

Crop this area

FIGURE D-8: Image cropped to scale and centered

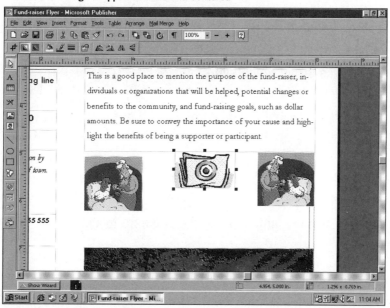

Recoloring an object

In addition to being cropped, images can be altered through recoloring. Once an object has been selected, right-click it, point to Change Picture, then click Recolor Picture (or click Format on the menu bar, then Recolor Picture). This method lets you change all the colors in the picture to different shades of a single color—ideal when creating a watermark effect. Figure D-9 shows the Recolor Picture dialog box.

FIGURE D-9: Recolor Picture dialog box

Click here for additional colors

Click to restore the original colors

Sample image is displayed here

Aligning and Grouping Images

Once you have inserted clip art, you can align multiple images so that the layout of the publication looks professionally designed. Artwork can be aligned from left to right or from top to bottom. Images can also be arranged in groups. A group makes it easy to move several pieces of art as one unit. Mary wants to make sure the three images on the page are precisely lined up. Then she will move them as a group.

Steps

1. Press and hold **[Shift]**, click the **right image**, click the **left image**, then release **[Shift]**

All three images should be selected, as shown in Figure D-10. You can use the shortcut menu to line up the objects.

2. Place the pointer over **one of the images**, right-click the **objects**, then click **Align Objects**

The Align Objects dialog box opens, as shown in Figure D-11. You want the objects lined up top to bottom along their centers.

> **QuickTip**
>
> You can also line up objects by selecting the objects, clicking Arrange on the menu bar, then clicking Align Objects.

3. Click the **Top to bottom Centers option button**, then click **OK**

Now that the images are all perfectly lined up, you can group them to make sure the alignment is preserved when you move them.

4. Click the **Group Objects button**

The three selected objects are transformed into a single selected object.

5. Drag the **selected grouped object** so that the lower edge of the frame is at 6½" V

Compare your work with Figure D-12. You don't always want to retain the group; you can always regroup later.

> **QuickTip**
>
> You can move selected grouped or ungrouped objects by pressing an arrow key (on the keyboard) while pressing and holding [Alt].

6. Click the **Ungroup Objects button**, then press **[F9]**

Save your work.

7. Click the **Save button** on the Standard toolbar

CLUES TO USE

Scanning artwork

If you have a favorite photo or piece of artwork that does not exist in electronic form, you can convert it to a digital computer file with a scanner. A variety of scanners are available, in either a hand-held or flatbed format. You can scan text, line art, or full-color images with amazing accuracy, enabling you to use virtually any image as clip art. Every scanner comes with its own easy-to-use imaging software. Publisher also lets you scan directly into a publication by clicking Insert on the menu bar, pointing to Picture, then clicking Scanner or Camera. The Picture menu commands appear dimmed unless a scanner or camera is installed on the computer.

FIGURE D-10: All three images selected

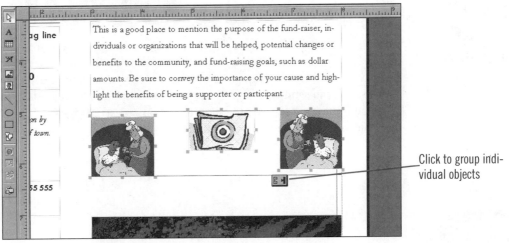

Click to group individual objects

FIGURE D-11: Align Objects dialog box

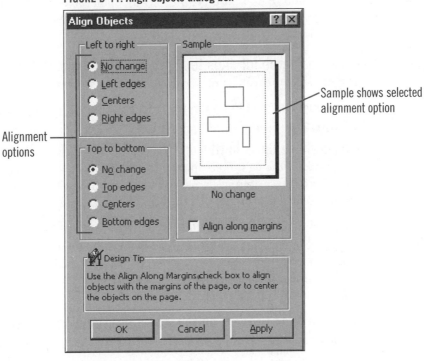

Alignment options

Sample shows selected alignment option

FIGURE D-12: Lined-up and grouped objects

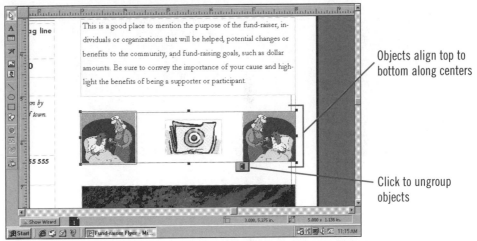

Objects align top to bottom along centers

Click to ungroup objects

Layering Objects

When positioning objects, you might want some images to appear in front of others. This layering effect can be used with any type of frame. You might want text to display on top of a shape, or you might want one image to overlap another image, with a text frame in front of both images. You can send an image to the back (so it appears to be underneath an object), or bring it to the front (so it appears to be on top of an object). ➤ Mary experiments with layering objects to improve the look of the flyer.

Steps

1. Click the **image** at **4" H/6" V**, press **[F9]**, click the **Clip Gallery Tool button** 🖼 on the Objects toolbar, then drag the + pointer from **2¾" H/5" V/ to 3½" H/6" V**
   You want an image to overlap the existing image.

2. Click the **Search for clips text box**, type **light bulb**, then press **[Enter]**
   The results of the search are displayed in the Insert Clip Art dialog box.

3. Right-click the **first image in the first row**, click **Clip Properties**, verify the filename as **BD04924_** in the Clip Properties dialog box, click **OK**, click the **image**, click 🔄, then click the **Close button** on the Insert Clip Art dialog box
   The image of the light bulb appears in the frame, as shown in Figure D-13. Using simple images, you can create unusual effects by changing the order of images on the page. If you send the light bulb image to the back, the original image looks as if it's on top of the light bulb.

4. Click the **Send to Back button** 🔲 on the Standard toolbar
   The image of the light bulb now looks as if it is behind the nurse and patient. See Figure D-14. This is an interesting effect, but it looked better with the light bulb in front. Notice that even though the light bulb appears to be behind the nurse and patient image, you can still see the handles for the light bulb image.

5. Click the **Bring to Front button** 🔲 on the Standard toolbar
   The light bulb appears in front of the nurse and patient, and you can save your work.

6. Click the **Save button** 🖫 on the Standard toolbar

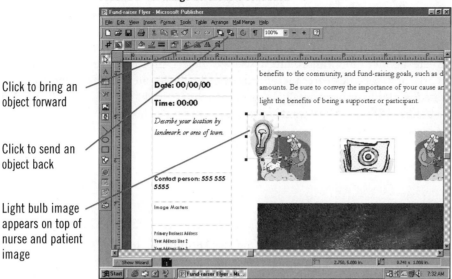

FIGURE D-13: Image before it is sent back

Click to bring an object forward

Click to send an object back

Light bulb image appears on top of nurse and patient image

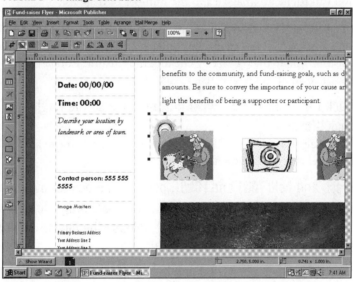

FIGURE D-14: Image sent back

Layering text on an object

By creatively layering text and objects, you can make text appear on top of objects. Figure D-15 shows a text frame on top of many geometric shapes. By cleverly using the Bring to Front and Send to Back buttons, you can superimpose the text frame on all the shapes. Otherwise the shapes could easily obscure the text frame. Some circles are in front of the burst, but behind the text frame. This effect is achieved using the Bring Forward and Send Backward commands on the Arrange menu. Unlike Bring to Front and Send to Back, these commands move an image forward or back one layer at a time.

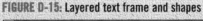

FIGURE D-15: Layered text frame and shapes

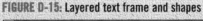

Rotating Art

The **rotation** of an image—measured in degrees from a horizontal plane—can be changed using the Rotate pointer. You can rotate a selected object in 15-degree increments by pressing [Alt][Ctrl], or in specific degree increments by using the Rotate Objects dialog box. Artwork can be rotated vertically or horizontally by using the Rotate Right button or the Rotate Left button on the toolbar. ✎ Mary wants to rotate an object on the page.

Steps

1. Click the **Rotate Right button** 🔳 on the Formatting toolbar
   The image of the light bulb rotates 90 degrees to the right. You decide to return the image to its original rotation.

2. Click the **Undo button** 🔳 on the Standard toolbar
   You can rotate an image a specific number of degrees.

QuickTip
You might find it helpful to move the Custom Rotate dialog box so you can see the object being rotated.

3. Click **Arrange** on the menu bar, point to **Rotate or Flip**, then click **Custom Rotate**
   The Custom Rotate dialog box opens, as shown in Figure D-16. You can also open the Custom Rotate dialog box by clicking the Custom Rotate button 🔳 on the Standard toolbar once an object is selected.

4. Click the **Counterclockwise button** twice so the Angle text box displays 10.0, then click **Close**
   The image is rotated 10 degrees counterclockwise. You can also rotate the image in 15-degree increments using the Rotator pointer.

5. Press and hold **[Alt]** and **[Ctrl]**, position the pointer over the top-left handle so that it changes to 🔳 ROTATE, as shown in Figure D-17, drag the 🔳 ROTATE pointer counterclockwise to rotate one increment to the left, release the mouse, then release **[Alt]** and **[Ctrl]**
   Compare your image with Figure D-18.

6. Press **[F9]**, then click the **Save button** 🔳 on the Standard toolbar
   You zoomed out and saved your changes.

FIGURE D-16: Custom Rotate dialog box

Each click rotates image 5 degrees counterclockwise

Enter a specific number of degrees

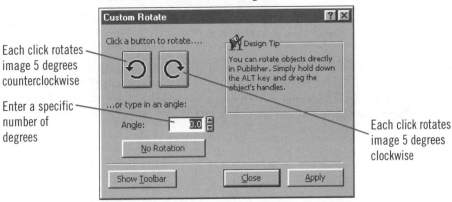

Each click rotates image 5 degrees clockwise

FIGURE D-17: Rotating an object in 15-degree increments

Rotate pointer

Outline shows new position

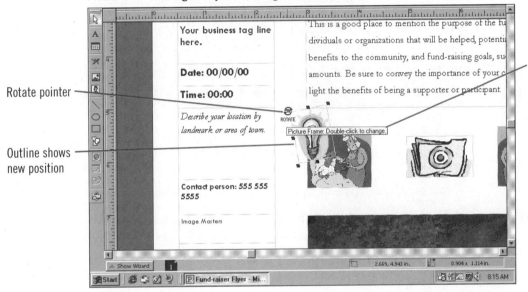

ScreenTips can be turned off with the View menu

FIGURE D-18: Rotated image

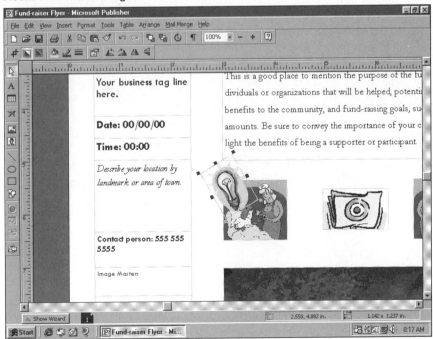

Publisher 2000

Using Drawing Tools

Publisher has a variety of drawing tools you can use to create your own geometric designs. The toolbox contains four drawing tools that let you draw lines, circles, rectangles, and custom shapes. Any shape drawn on a page can be moved, resized, or formatted to meet your personal design specifications. Shapes created with drawing tools can be flipped as well as rotated. Mary wants to fill an empty space with an original geometric design. She begins by drawing a border to frame the design.

Steps

1. Click the **Rectangle Tool button** ▢ on the Objects toolbar
   You can create a shape by dragging the pointer to the size you need.

2. **Drag the + pointer from 6½" H/½" V to 8" H/1¾" V, then press [F9]**
   The rectangular box is drawn on the page. You can add interesting shapes, such as a thunderbolt, using the Custom Shapes button.

3. Click the **Custom Shapes button** 🖫 on the Objects toolbar, click the **thunderbolt** (the fifth shape from the left in the last row), then drag the + pointer from 7½" H/¼" V to 8" H/1¾" V
   You want to flip this shape so it points toward the masthead.

   QuickTip

   If you want to repeat a designed shape, create one with all the formatting attributes you want, then copy and paste it.

4. Click the **Flip Horizontal button** ◣ on the Formatting toolbar
   Compare your drawing to Figure D-19. You see how easy it is to create interesting and professional-looking design elements in a publication.

5. Click 🖫, click the **fifth burst** in the fourth row, then drag the + pointer from 6½" H/¾" V to 8" H/1¾" V
   Compare your work to Figure D-20. Using custom shapes, you can create logos and a variety of design elements to enhance your publication.

6. Click the **Save button** 🖫 on the Standard toolbar

FIGURE D-19: Drawing a custom shape

Click to open palette of custom shapes

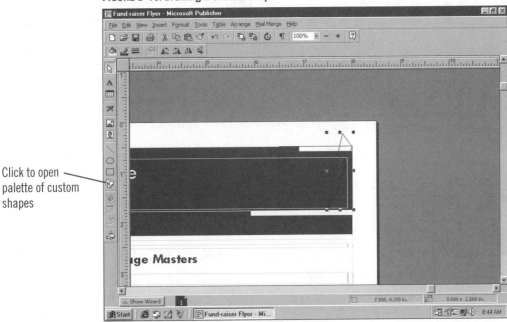

FIGURE D-20: Design created with drawing tools

Mirrored image

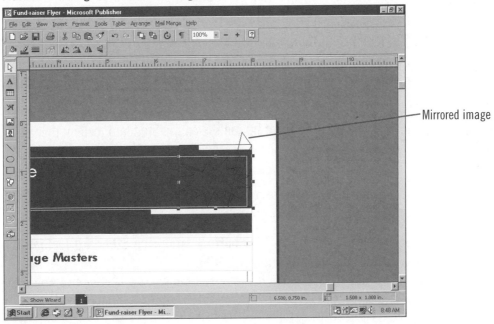

CLUES TO USE

Drawing perfect shapes and lines

Sometimes you want to draw an exact shape or line. To draw a square, click the Rectangle Tool ▭, then press and hold [Shift] as you drag the ＋ pointer. Press and hold [Shift] to create a circle using the Oval Tool ○. Press and hold [Shift] to create a horizontal, vertical, or 45-degree angle straight line using the Line Tool ◣. To center an object at a specific location, click the tool to create the object, place the pointer where you want the center of the object to be, then hold [Ctrl] as you drag the mouse. Remember to always release the mouse button before you release the [Ctrl] or [Shift] key.

Fill Drawn Shapes

Drawn shapes can be left with their default attributes—displaying whatever background exists—or you can fill them using a variety of colors and patterns. Colors and patterns enhance designs and help you create elegant original graphics in your publication. Dialog boxes for colors and patterns can be accessed from the menu bar or by using a button on the Formatting toolbar. Mary would like to add color and patterns to the shapes in her design. She begins by adding color to the burst.

1. Make sure the **burst** is still selected, click the **Fill Color button** 🖫 on the Formatting toolbar, then click **Accent 3 (Orange)**
The burst becomes orange. You can add color and patterns to the thunderbolt to make it stand out.

2. Click the **thunderbolt**, click **Format** on the menu bar, point to **Fill Color**, click **More Colors**, then make sure the **Basic colors option button** is selected
The Colors dialog box opens, as shown in Figure D-21.

3. Click the **Yellow row box 10 (Gold)**, then click **OK**
You can add patterns to the object.

4. Click **Format** on the menu bar, point to **Fill Color**, then click **Fill Effects**
The Fill Effects dialog box opens, as shown in Figure D-22.

5. Click the **90% shade pattern box** to the right of the current selection, then click **OK**
Bringing the thunderbolt forward can add dimension to the design.

6. Click the **Bring to Front button** 🖫 on the Standard toolbar, then click the **workspace** to deselect the object
Compare your work to Figure D-23. Zoom out to see the whole publication, then save your work.

7. Press **[F9]**, click the **text frame at 1" H/6½" V**, press **[F9]**, select the **Contact Person text**, then type *your name*

8. Press **[F9]**, click the **Save button** 🖫 on the Standard toolbar, then click the **Print button** 🖫 on the Standard toolbar
The art is well placed in the flyer. You can go back later and complete the text frames.

9. Exit Publisher

FIGURE D-21: Colors dialog box

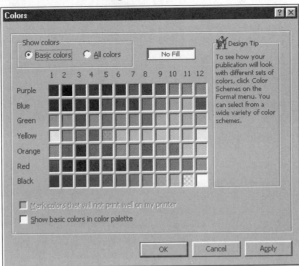

FIGURE D-22: Fill Effects dialog box

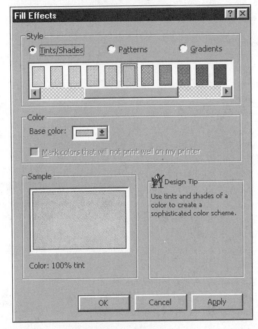

FIGURE D-23: Formatting applied to objects

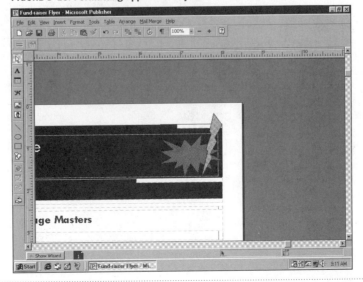

Practice

► Concepts Review

Label each of the elements of the Publisher window shown in Figure D-24.

FIGURE D-24

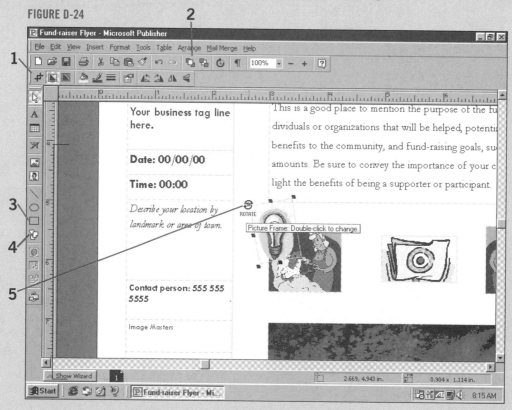

Match each of the terms with the statement that describes its function.

6. ▣

7. ▣

8. ▣

9. Clip Gallery

10. ✛ CROP

11. ⟲ ROTATE

a. Contains ClipArt

b. Sends an object behind another

c. Conceals part(s) of images

d. Brings an object forward

e. Rotator pointer

f. Creates a custom shape

Select the best answer from the list of choices.

12. Create a square using the Rectangle Tool button by holding
   a. [Ctrl]
   b. [Alt]
   c. [Shift]
   d. [Esc]

13. You can do each of the following with ClipArt, *except*
    a. rotate.
    b. italicize.
    c. flip.
    d. crop.

14. Which button *cannot* be used with ClipArt?
    a. [B]
    b. [⬛]
    c. [⬛]
    d. [⬛]

15. Rotate an object in 15-degree increments by holding
    a. [Ctrl][Shift]
    b. [Alt][Ctrl]
    c. [Alt][Shift]
    d. [Esc]

16. To resize an object, maintaining its scale while dragging, hold
    a. [Shift]
    b. [Alt][Shift]
    c. [Ctrl]
    d. [Alt]

17. Which pointer is used to drag a custom shape?
    a. ⬛
    b. +
    c. ⬛
    d. ⬛

18. To create a circle, click the _____ button then press and hold [Shift] while dragging the pointer.
    a. [▢]
    b. [◯]
    c. [◣]
    d. [▦]

19. Which pointer is used to copy an object *without* placing a copy on the Clipboard?
    a. ⬛
    b. ⬛
    c. ⬛
    d. +

20. Which button is used to add colors and patterns to objects?
    a. [⬛]
    b. [⬛]
    c. [⬛]
    d. [⬛]

Skills Review

1. Insert and resize clip art.

a. Start Publisher.

b. Use the Catalog's Postcards Wizard to create a postcard for a family picnic. Select the Art Boxes Invitation Postcard with the Mountain color scheme, use the Secondary Personal Information set, and accept all other defaults.

c. Save the file on your Project Disk as Family Picnic Postcard.

d. Use the Clip Gallery tool to draw a picture frame from 4¼" H/1½" V to 4¾" H/2" V.

e. Search the Clip Gallery for clips using the word "picnic."

f. Locate the image of a picnicking senior couple (the image's filename, PE02622_.WMF, can be verified in Properties).

g. Insert the image, then close the Insert Clip Art dialog box.

h. Zoom into the image, then resize by placing the pointer over the upper-left handle, then dragging the frame to 1½" V.

i. Save your work.

2. Copy and move an object.

a. Copy the selected image using the Clipboard.

b. Paste the image on the publication. (Throughout this section, zoom in and out whenever necessary.)

c. Move the newly pasted copy to the left side of the page, so the bottom-left edge is at 1½" H/2" V.

d. Flip the copy using the Flip Horizontal button.

e. Save your work.

3. Crop an image.

a. Use the Clip Gallery Tool and draw a frame from 2¾" H/2½" V to 3½" H/3" V.

b. Search for clips using the word "picnic."

c. Locate the black and white image of three people at a picnic table (filename PE00833_.WMF), insert the image, then close the Insert Clip Art dialog box.

d. Click the Crop Picture button on the Formatting toolbar.

e. Crop the right edge of the image so the person on the left and table remain in the image (at 3³⁄₁₆").

f. Turn off the cropping pointer.

g. Resize the image while retaining its proportions by dragging the corner handle, so its new upper-right edge is at 3¼" H.

h. Save your work.

4. Align and group images.

   a. Select the two clip art images of the picnicking couple.

   b. Open the Align Objects dialog box and line up the objects, using the top edges.

   c. Group the objects.

   d. Move the object so the top edge is at 1½" V.

   e. Ungroup the object.

   f. Save the publication.

5. Layer objects.

   a. Use the Clip Gallery Tool and draw a frame from 3" H/2⅜" V to 3½" H/2¾" V.

   b. Search for clips using the word picnic.

   c. Locate the picnic basket and sunshine image (filename FD00306_.WMF), insert the image, then close the Insert Clip Art dialog box.

   d. Send the new image behind the cropped image.

   e. Bring the object to the front.

   f. Save the publication.

6. Rotate art.

   a. Rotate the selected image 15 degrees using the Rotate toolbar button.

   b. Move the selected image down, so that the top-right handle is at 2⅜" V.

   c. Deselect the image.

   d. Save the publication.

7. Use drawing tools.

   a. Use the Custom Shapes button to create a right-pointing arrow from 1¾" H/2½" V to 2¼" H/3" V.

   b. Zoom in to the arrow.

   c. Create a copy of this shape and drag it to the upper left corner to 4" H/2½" V.

   d. Click the Flip Horizontal button.

   e. Save your work.

8. Fill drawn shapes.

   a. Change the color of the selected shape to Accent 1 (Medium Blue).

   b. Change the Fill Effect to 50% tint.

   c. Click the Format Painter button, then click the right-pointing arrow (at 2" H/2½" V).

   d. Replace the name Carlos Mendoza (in the e-mail address) with your own name.

   e. Save your work.

   f. Print the first page of the publication and hand in your work.

   g. Exit Publisher.

Independent Challenges

1. Image Masters is considering a new layout for its business cards, and they have asked you to come up with a possible design.

To complete this independent challenge:

a. Start Publisher if necessary, use the (Plain Paper) Scallops Business Card Catalog Wizard with a Landscape orientation, a logo placeholder, one card in the center of the page, and the Secondary Business Personal Information set.

b. Change the color scheme to Tidepool.

c. Save the publication as New IM Card Design on your Project Disk.

d. Replace the existing logo with the IM logo (on your Project Disk), using the Smart Object Wizard button.

e. Add your e-mail address in the space provided beneath the fax number.

f. Use at least three drawing tools to create an interesting series of shapes in the upper-right corner of the business card. Change the Fill Color and Fill Effects of at least two of the shapes.

g. If desired, rotate and layer the artwork.

h. Save the publication.

i. Print the publication.

j. Exit Publisher.

2. A local clothing store has asked you to use your design skills to create a gift certificate for a new sales promotion. To complete this independent challenge:

a. Start Publisher, use the Mobile Special Gift Certificate Catalog Wizard, and accept all the wizard defaults.

b. Save the publication as Gift Certificate on your Project Disk.

c. Click the Clip Gallery Tool and create a frame at ½" H/2¼" V to 1¼" H/3" V.

d. Add artwork of your own choosing.

e. If necessary, crop the clip art to best suit your publication.

f. Add objects created with drawing tools, and add color and patterns if appropriate. If necessary, resize any drawn objects.

g. Create a text frame above the "This certificate entitles" text, then type your name in the frame.

h. Save and print the publication.

i. Exit Publisher.

3. You've decided to spruce up your work area, and a customized calendar is just what you need. To complete this independent challenge:

a. Start Publisher if necessary, use the (Full Page) Blends Calendar Catalog Wizard for the current month and year, and accept all the wizard defaults.

b. Change the Personal Information to the Secondary Business Personal Information set.

c. Change the color scheme to one of your own choosing.

d. Save the publication as Current Calendar on your Project Disk.

e. If desired, add clip art to the page.

f. Add objects created with drawing tools, and add color and patterns if appropriate. If necessary, resize any drawn objects.

g. Replace the name Carlos Mendoza (in the e-mail address) with your own name.

h. Save and print the publication.

i. Exit Publisher.

4. Your new client, Luggable Luggage, has hired you to design its new Web site. Using your Internet skills, you find other luggage sites before you begin your assignment.
To complete this independent challenge:

a. Connect to the Internet and use your browser and favorite search engine to find other luggage sites.

b. Print out the home pages from at least two sites that feature luggage sales. Take note of their use of graphic images.

c. Disconnect from the Internet.

d. Start Publisher, then use the Catalog to create a single-page Web site using any design you choose.

e. Save it on your Project Disk as Luggable Luggage.

f. Replace the default artwork, using clip art or drawn shapes.

g. Add appropriate text (if necessary) to describe the artwork. (Add your name somewhere on the page.)

h. Format the artwork, using your Publisher skills, by cropping any undesirable elements from the image, or adding formatting and colors to drawn shapes.

i. Copy and align images to enhance the publication.

j. Save the publication.

k. Print the publication.

l. Exit Publisher.

▶ Visual Workshop

Use the Catalog to create the Layered Bars Invitation (use the invitation category in the Postcards Wizard). Save this publication on your Project Disk as Party Invitation. Use Figure D-25 as a guide. Change the color scheme to Sunset, and substitute your name for Mary Garrott (as shown in the figure in the e-mail address). Replace all text as shown in the figure, update the Personal Information (if necessary), and add drawn objects. Save and print the flyer.

FIGURE D-25

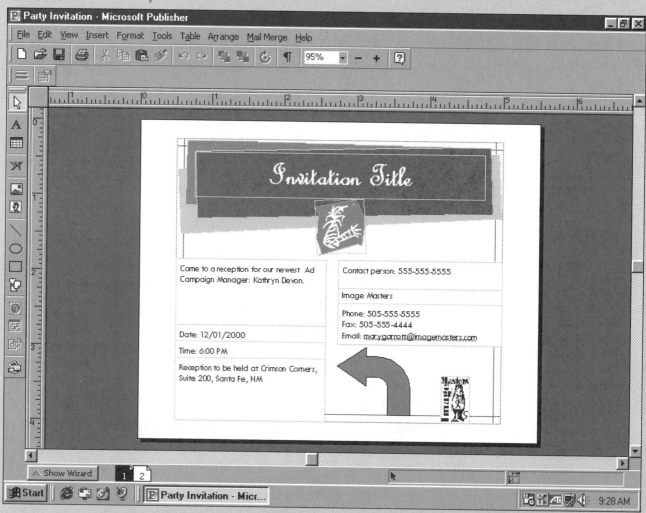

Enhancing

a Publication

Objectives

- ► **Define styles**
- ► **Modify and apply a style**
- ► **Change a format into a style**
- ► **Create columns**
- ► **Adjust text overflows**
- ► **Add Continued on/from notices**
- ► **Add drop caps**
- ► **Create reversed text**

Text within a publication must be easy to read. Professionals advise you not to use more than two fonts per page, because too many fonts make a page look busy and detract from the publication's message. Formatting a limited number of fonts in different sizes, with bold or italics, can add to the visual interest without creating confusion. Story text can be in one or more columns, depending on the desired layout. Story text that does not fit within a single text frame on a page can be continued elsewhere in a publication. Publisher has tools to help map and link the frames to create a cohesive publication. ✐ Michael Ravenwood is the account executive for an Image Masters' client, *Route 66 Traveler*, a monthly newsletter. He is laying out the text for an upcoming issue.

Defining Styles

The appearance of text in a publication determines its legibility. Text that is too large looks awkward; text that is too small or fancy looks busy and can be hard to read. You can easily provide consistency within the text by using styles. A **style** is a defined set of text formatting attributes, such as a font, font size, and paragraph alignment. Creating a style means that all the text in a publication can have a consistent look. ✎▬▬ Michael creates a newsletter using the Catalog and defines a style that he will use throughout the publication.

Steps 1234

1. Start Publisher, click **Newsletters** in the Wizards list, click **Voyage Newsletter**, click **Start Wizard**, then click **Finish** (if necessary)
   The Newsletter appears on the screen.

2. Click **Personal Information** in the Newsletter Wizard, click the **Secondary Business option button**, click **Update**, then, if necessary, change the entries to **Carlos Mendoza** in the Name text box, **Account Executive** in the title text box, **Image Masters, Crimson Corner Suite 200, Santa Fe, NM, 87501** in the Address text box, **Phone: 505-555-5555, Fax: 505-555-4444, Email** *carlos.mendoza@imagemasters.com*, in the Phone/fax/e-mail text box, **Image Masters** in the Organization name text box, **We make you look your best** in the Tag line text box, then click **Update**

3. Click **Color Scheme** in the Newsletter Wizard, click **Citrus** in the Color Scheme list, click the **Hide Wizard button** ▼ Hide Wizard , then save the publication as **Route 66 Traveler** on your Project Disk
   Publisher comes with some text styles, or you can create your own text styles. You can see existing styles using the Text Style dialog box.

4. Click **Format** on the menu bar, then click **Text Style**
   The Text Style dialog box opens, as shown in Figure E-1. This dialog box lets you modify existing styles and create new ones. You can create a style that can be used in other paragraphs in this publication.

5. Click the **Click to Create a new style button** ▣ in the Text Style dialog box
   The Create New Style dialog box opens, as shown in Figure E-2. You can change the type size of the font, change the line and character spacing, adjust the tabs, and even modify the alignment. By naming the new style you make it available for use.

6. Type **Route 66 paragraph** in the Enter new style name text box, click the **Click to change Character type and size button** ▣ , click the **Size list arrow** in the Font dialog box, click **14**, then click **OK**
   The Route 66 paragraph style will have a font that is 14 points.

7. Click the **Click to change Indents and lists button** ▣ , click the **Alignment list arrow** in the Indents and Lists dialog box, click **Center**, then click **OK**
   The sample in the Create New Style dialog box displays how the new style will look.

8. Click **OK** in the Create New Style dialog box
   The new style appears in the list of existing styles, as shown in Figure E-3.

9. Click **Close** in the Text Style dialog box, then click the **Save button** ▣ on the Standard toolbar
   Now the style can be applied to text in the publication.

FIGURE E-1: Text Style dialog box

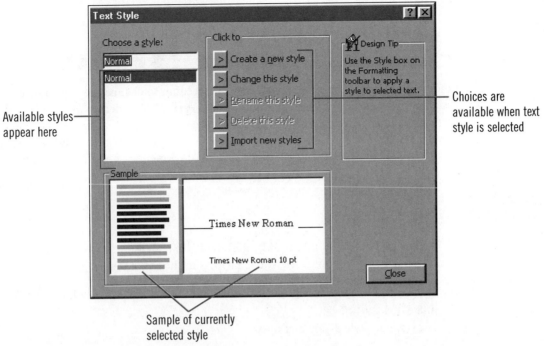

Available styles appear here

Choices are available when text style is selected

Sample of currently selected style

FIGURE E-2: Create New Style dialog box

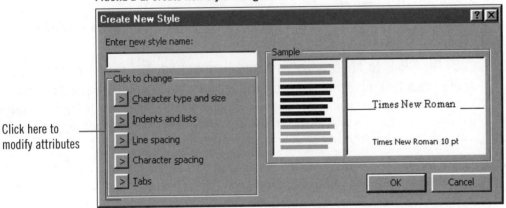

Click here to modify attributes

FIGURE E-3: New style in Text Style dialog box

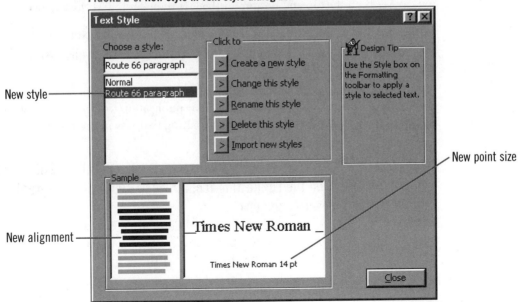

New style

New point size

New alignment

Modifying and Applying a Style

Since any style can be modified, you have the freedom to change the appearance of all the text assigned to a specific style within a publication, easily. If you decide to change a style, you can reapply the modified style to reformat text. Once you've defined a style, you can apply it to text so your publication develops a consistent look with similar attributes. ✒️━━ Michael modifies the style he just created, then inserts a Word document and applies the defined style to it.

Steps

1. Click **Format** on the menu bar, then click **Text Style**
   Route 66 paragraph, the style you created, is in the list of styles.

2. Click **Route 66 paragraph** in the Choose a style list, then click the **Click to Change this style button** ▸
   The Change Style dialog box opens.

3. Click the **Click to change Character type and size button** ▸, click the **Size list arrow**, click **12**, then click **OK**
   You changed the font size for the Route 66 paragraph style from 14 point to 12 point. The change appears in the sample.

4. Click the **Click to change Indents and lists button** ▸, click the **Alignment list arrow**, click **Left**, click **OK**, then click **OK** to close the Change Style dialog box
   The modified text size and alignment should appear in the Text Style dialog box, as shown in Figure E-4. Any new and existing text that has the Route 66 paragraph style applied to it will look consistent with text already in the publication.

5. Click **Close** to close the Text Style dialog box
   Working on text is easier when you zoom in to see the frames.

6. Click the **text frame at 3" H/5" V**, then click the **Zoom In button** ⊞ until 66% appears in the Zoom box on the Standard toolbar
   You can see both the top and bottom of the text frame in the workspace window.

QuickTip

If you choose not to use the Autoflow feature, the extra text can be adjusted manually.

7. Right-click the **text frame**, click **Delete Text**, click **Insert** on the menu bar, click **Text File**, locate your Project Disk, click **PUB E-1**, click **OK**, then click **No** in the warning box to not use autoflow
   Using the Autoflow feature automatically takes text that doesn't fit in a frame and places it in the next available text frame. Compare your publication to Figure E-5. The inserted text is in the Arial font at 12-point size, the formatting that was in the original text document. You can apply a paragraph style to this text.

8. Right-click the **text frame**, point to **Change text**, click **Highlight Entire Story**, click the **Style list arrow** on the Formatting toolbar, click **Route 66 paragraph**, then click the **text frame** to deselect the text
   Before you applied the new style, the Font and Font Size text boxes were blank, indicating that more than one font and size were selected. Compare your page to Figure E-6. The text is now Times New Roman, 12 point, and left-justified.

9. Click the **Zoom Out button** ⊟ twice, then save your publication

FIGURE E-4: Text size changed in Text Style dialog box

New style attributes
appear here

FIGURE E-5: Word file inserted into text frame

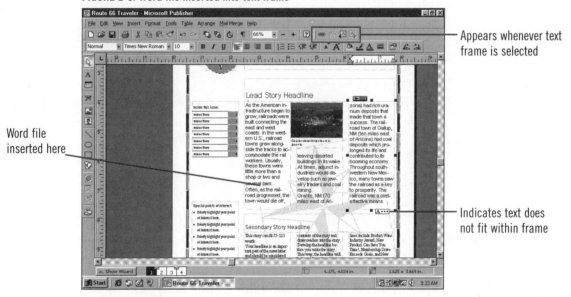

Appears whenever text
frame is selected

Word file
inserted here

Indicates text does
not fit within frame

FIGURE E-6: Style applied to text in frame

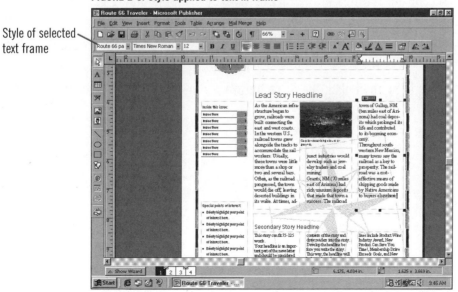

Style of selected
text frame

Publisher 2000

Changing a Format into a Style

A style can be created from formatted text within a text frame. This means that without knowing all the attributes that make up a text's appearance, you can turn it into a style. This process is called creating a **style by example**. Formatted text can be used to create a style by selecting the text then typing a name in the Style list box on the Formatting toolbar. Creating a style by example makes the style available for use over and over again in the publication. The difference between using a style and using the Format painter is that the Format painter button reformats selected characters according to the style of currently selected characters, but does not store or name the style. Michael likes the style created by the wizard for the story titles and wants to create a style from this format that he can use throughout the publication.

Steps 1234

1. Click the **Lead Story Headline text**, then press **[F9]**
   The Lead Story Headline is selected and visible on your screen.

2. Click **Normal** in the Style list box on the Formatting toolbar
   The current style—in this case, Normal—is selected, as shown in Figure E-7. You name styles so that you can identify their use easily.

3. Type **Route 66 heading** in the Style list box, then press **[Enter]**
   The Create Style By Example dialog box opens, as shown in Figure E-8. To create a style based on the current formatting of the selected text in the Lead Story headline, you entered a name in the Style list box. The Sample box shows you the current style's font and size, as well as its alignment setting.

4. Click **OK**
   The Create Style By Example dialog box closes. Notice that the new name, Route 66 heading, appears in the Style list box on the Formatting toolbar.

5. Make sure the entire **Lead Story Headline** is selected, then type **Western Town Growth**
   You can now use this style anywhere in the publication.

6. Click anywhere within the **Newsletter Title text**, click **Normal** in the Style list box on the Formatting toolbar, type **Route 66 masthead**, press **[Enter]**, then click **OK** to accept the settings in the Create Style By Example dialog box
   You can now use this style anywhere in the publication.

7. Make sure the entire **Newsletter Title** is selected, then type **Route 66 Traveler**
   Compare your publication to Figure E-9.

8. Press **[F9]**, then click the **Save button** 🖫 on the Standard toolbar

FIGURE E-7: Style selected in the Style list box

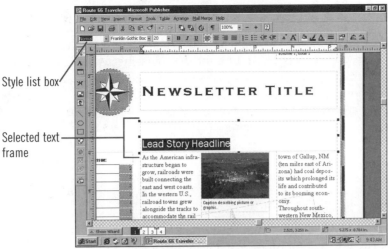

Style list box

Selected text frame

FIGURE E-8: Create Style By Example dialog box

Current alignment

Current font and size

FIGURE E-9: New style name appears in Style list box

New style name

CLUES TO USE

Adjusting spaces between characters

Sometimes characters don't look quite right when they're printed: they may seem packed too close together or spread too far apart. Adjusting the spacing between character pairs, or **kerning**, can make text look better. The characters A W R Y might have more space between the letters A, W, R, and Y than you want. You can kern these characters so there is less space between the characters, so that it now looks this way: AWRY. Publisher automatically kerns characters having point sizes greater than 14, but you can kern any characters you choose by selecting the character pair(s) to be adjusted, clicking Format on the menu bar, then clicking Character Spacing. You can change scaling, tracking, and kerning of characters using the Character Spacing dialog box shown in Figure E-10.

FIGURE E-10: Character Spacing dialog box

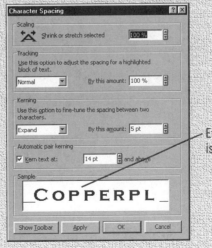

Effect of spacing option is displayed here

Publisher 2000

Publisher 2000

Creating Columns

Most newsletter stories are formatted in multiple columns to give them a more professional look. When you create a publication using the Newsletter Wizard, a page may display a three-column layout, but you can use the wizard to change the layout to more or fewer columns. The wizard lets you choose whether you want to change the layout of the left- or right-hand page, and lets you choose from 1 to 3 columns. ➤ Michael wants to see how columns can be better arranged on page 3. He also replaces the graphic placeholder with another image.

Steps

1. Click the **2-3 page icon** on the horizontal status bar
   The Newsletter Wizard lets you easily change a page's layout.

2. Click the **Show Wizard button** `Show Wizard`, click **Number of Columns** in the Newsletter Wizard, click the **How many columns would you like on this page? list arrow** in the Number of Columns wizard pane, then click **Right Inside Page**
   Your screen should look like Figure E-11. You would like to see how the right inside page looks with 2 columns.

3. Click the **2 columns option button**
   In a few seconds, the layout of page 3, the right inside page, changes to 2 columns. You can return to the original layout using the wizard.

4. Click the **3 columns option button**, then click the **Hide Wizard button** `Hide Wizard`
   The page returns to its original 3-column layout. Columns wrap around the image, and the placeholder graphic image can easily be replaced with an image on your disk.

5. Click the **graphic image** at **12" H/4" V**, press **[F9]**, right-click the **image**, point to **Change Picture**, point to **Picture**, click **From File**, locate **Sunset.tif** on your Project Disk, then click **Insert**
   The new image replaces the placeholder.

6. Click the **caption placeholder text**, click **Normal** in the Style list box on the Formatting toolbar, type **Route 66 caption**, press **[Enter]**, then click **OK** to close the Create Style By Example dialog box
   This caption style will be applied to other captions in the publication.

7. Type **Sunset along Route 66**
   Compare your publication with Figure E-12.

8. Press **[F9]**, then click the **Save button** 🖫 on the Standard toolbar

FIGURE E-11: Newsletter Wizard column layout options

Click to change
from left
to right
inside pages

Click to change
layout

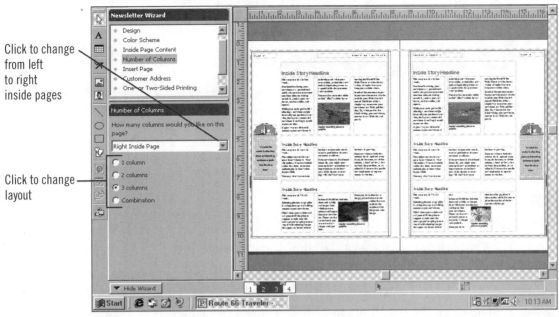

FIGURE E-12: Placeholder image and caption replaced

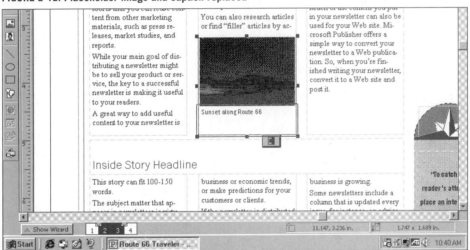

Manually creating multiple columns

You can use the Text Frame Tool button A to create a single column. You can create multiple columns within a single text frame by changing the frame's properties. Using the Text Frame Properties dialog box, shown in Figure E-13, a frame can be modified to contain multiple columns of equal widths. This allows multiple columns to exist within a single text frame. Multiple text frames can also be created and placed adjacent to one another, to give the appearance of columns.

FIGURE E-13: Text Frame Properties dialog box

Indicate the
number of
columns here

Distance
between
columns

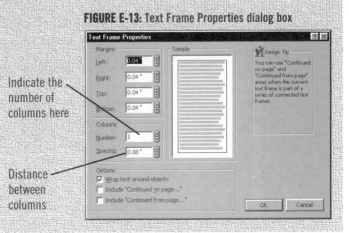

Adjusting Text Overflows

Text does not always fit neatly within a text frame on one page. In some situations, such as a newsletter, you may want to have more than one story begin on one page and continue on others. Publisher makes it easy to take the overflow from one text frame and pour it into another text frame, using the Connect button at the bottom of the frame. A series of helpful pointers determine how and where you distribute the text throughout the frames in the publication. Various buttons and pointers help identify and navigate connected frames. ✒️ Michael places the overflow text from a story on page 1 into a frame on page 3.

Steps 1234

1. Right-click the text frame at **10" H/3" V**, click **Delete Text**, click the **page 1 icon**, right-click the text frame at **3" H/9" V**, then click **Delete Text**
   You wrote a long Word document that can be inserted into the frame on page 1.

> **QuickTip**
>
> Break a link between connected frames by clicking 🔗.

2. Right-click the text frame at **3" H/9" V**, point to **Change Text**, click **Text File**, locate your Project Disk, click **PUB E-2**, click **OK**, then click **No** when prompted to use autoflow
   The Text in Overflow button **A•••** at the bottom of the frame indicates that there is overflow text. Text that does not fit in this frame can be continued—using the 🏺 and 🏺 pointers—in other text frames. Frames that have text poured into them are linked to the previous frame. You want to pour this text into the frame on page 3.

3. Click the **Connect Text Frames button** 🔗 on the Standard toolbar, as shown in Figure E-14
   The pointer changes to 🏺 when placed on the workspace. This is the "pitcher" of text that you will pour into the next frame. When you place this pitcher over a text frame, it changes to a pouring pitcher 🏺, indicating that you can pour the text into the frame. You want the overflow to begin pouring on page 3.

> **Trouble?**
>
> If additional overflow remained (indicated by the appearance of the Text in Overflow button), you would repeat this process until no overflow text remained.

4. Click the **page 2-3 icon**, position the pointer at **10" H/3" V**, click the **frame** with the **pouring pitcher pointer** 🏺, then press **[F9]**
   Compare your page to Figure E-15. You can view your work as a single-page spread.

5. Press **[F9]**, click **View** on the menu bar, then click **Two-Page Spread**
   Only page 3 is visible. You might want to switch between single-page and two-page spread views to get a better look at those objects with which you're working. Clicking the Go To Previous Frame button is a fast way to jump to the previous connecting frame.

6. Right-click the workspace at **10" H/3"V**, then click **Undo Two-Page Spread**
   Compare your work to Figure E-16.

7. Click the **Save button** 💾 on the Standard toolbar

FIGURE E-14: Preparing to click the Connect Frames button

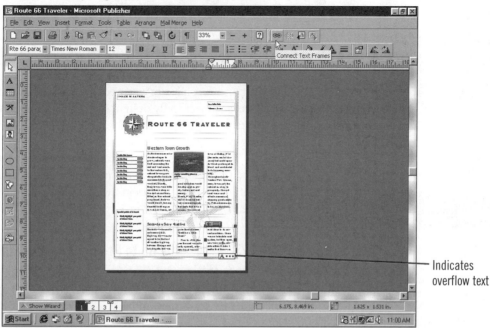

Indicates overflow text

FIGURE E-15: Overflow text poured into frame

Go to Previous Frame button

Go to Next Frame button

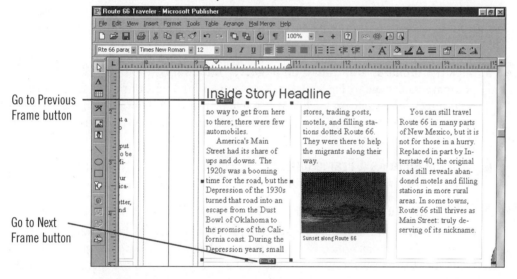

FIGURE E-16: Two-page spread with overflow text

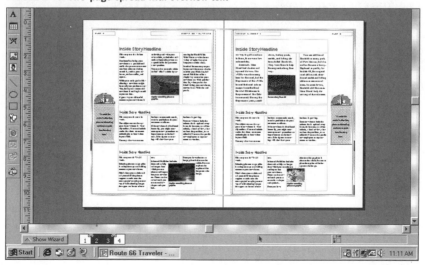

Adding Continued on/from Notices

When it is not possible to start and finish a story on the same page, "continued" notices can be added. Sometimes, publications are specifically designed with stories spanning several pages, to encourage readers to see all the pages in the publication. Because you want it to be as easy as possible to find and read all segments of a story, Publisher makes it easy to create **Continued on** and **Continued from** notices. These notices automatically insert text with the correct page reference—and references automatically update if you move the text frame. Michael inserts Continued on and Continued from notices in the story that spans two pages. He returns to page 1, the beginning of the story.

Steps

1. Click the frame at **10" H/3" V**, click the **Go to Previous Frame button** at the top of the frame, then press **[F9]**

The text frame is enlarged. You want the first Continued on notice to appear at the bottom of this text frame, since the text continues on page 3. You create a Continued on notice by modifying the text frame's properties.

2. Click **Format** on the menu bar, then click **Text Frame Properties**

The Text Frame Properties dialog box opens, as shown in Figure E-17. Check boxes in the Options area of the Text Frame Properties dialog box create Continued on/Continued from notices.

Trouble?

Continued on/from notices appear only if they refer to text on pages other than the current page.

3. Click the **Include "Continued on page..." check box**, then click **OK**

Compare your page to Figure E-18. You want to insert a Continued from notice at the beginning of the story on page 3. If a single text frame is continued from one page and continues on another page, you can insert the Continued on and Continued from notices at the same time.

4. Click the **Go to Next Frame button** at the bottom of the frame

Page 3 displays the continuation of the story.

QuickTip

Continued on/from notices must be turned on for each text frame. A single text frame containing multiple columns can turn on both notices in one step.

5. Right-click the **selected text frame**, point to **Change Frame**, click **Text Frame Properties**, click the **Include "Continued from page..." check box**, then click **OK**

The Continued from notice is displayed at the beginning of the text frame, as shown in Figure E-19. Continued on/from notices make a story take up more space on a page, adding several lines to its length.

6. Click the **Save button** on the Standard toolbar

FIGURE E-17: Text Frame Properties dialog box

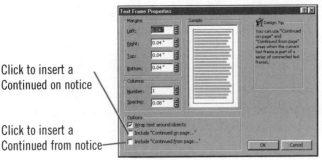

Click to insert a
Continued on notice

Click to insert a
Continued from notice

FIGURE E-18: Continued on notice

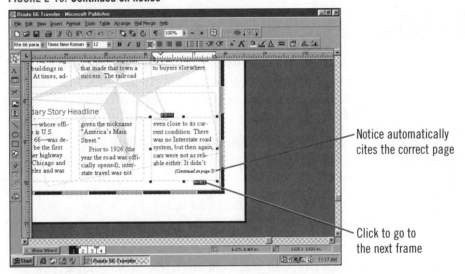

Notice automatically
cites the correct page

Click to go to
the next frame

FIGURE E-19: Continued from notice

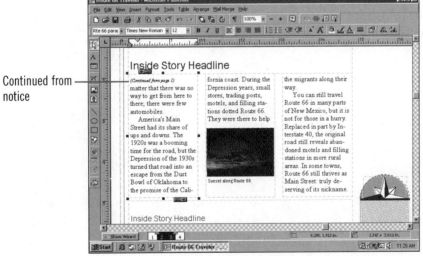

Continued from
notice

Changing the appearance of continued notices

If the appearance of a Continued on or Continued from notice does not appeal to you, it can be changed. Each type of continued notice has a defined style—you can see the style name in the Style list box. Change the style of a continued notice by selecting the notice you want to change, making formatting modifications, clicking the style name in the Style list box, then pressing [Enter].

Adding Drop Caps

In addition to using defined styles to give stories a consistent look, you can also add a **drop cap**, a large fancy first letter at the beginning of text. A drop cap can occur wherever you choose: at the beginning of each paragraph in a story, or only at the beginning of the story. Publisher lets you choose from defined character types that use different fonts and line heights, or you can create your own. Michael wants to dress up several stories using drop caps. He starts by applying a predefined drop cap to the story he just worked on.

Steps

1. Click the **Go To Previous Frame button** at the top of the selected frame, then click **anywhere in the first paragraph**
   You can apply a fancy letter to the initial character in the first paragraph of a story to make it stand out.

2. Click **Format** on the menu bar, then click **Drop Cap**
   The Drop Cap dialog box opens, as shown in Figure E-20. Because the addition of drop caps adds to the length of a story, they may cause the story to overflow.

3. Click the **Custom Drop Cap tab**
   You can change the default drop cap height to make the story fit its frame. You want a drop cap that is two lines high.

4. Click **Dropped letter position and size**, double-click the **Size of letters text box**, type **2**, as shown in Figure E-21, then click **OK**
   Compare your work to Figure E-22.

5. Click the **Save button** on the Standard toolbar
   Your work is saved with the modifications.

FIGURE E-20: Drop Cap dialog box

Indicates plain text

List of choices may look different

Scroll to see more choices

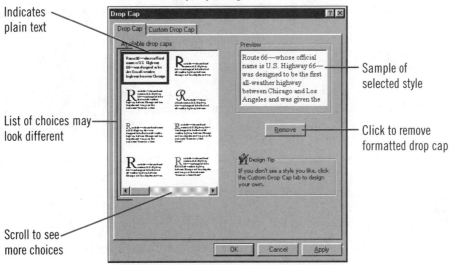

Sample of selected style

Click to remove formatted drop cap

FIGURE E-21: Creating a custom drop cap

Determines the letter's position

Controls the character's height

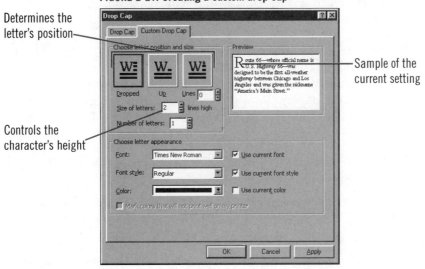

Sample of the current setting

FIGURE E-22: Drop cap added

Drop cap added

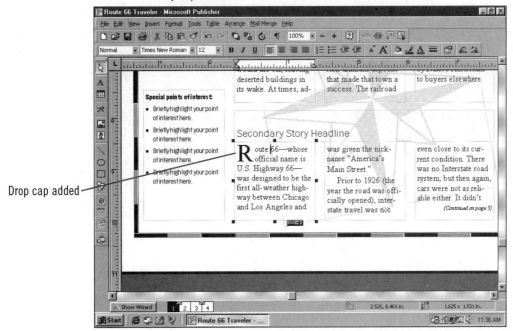

Creating Reversed Text

Another way to add emphasis to text—particularly titles—is to create reversed text. **Reversed text** is displayed as light characters on a dark background. This format makes the text look as though it was cut out of the background. Selecting all the text within the title's frame, then using buttons on the Formatting toolbar to change the colors of the font and the object creates this effect. ◤ Michael wants to create the effect of reversed text in the secondary story headline on the first page.

Steps 1 2 3 4

1. Click the **Secondary Story Headline text** just above the drop cap

2. Type **America's Main Street**
   The headline text is replaced, as shown in Figure E-23. Changing the font color is just one step in creating reversed text.

3. Press **[Ctrl][A]**, click the **Font Color button** 🅰 on the Formatting toolbar, then click the **Accent5 (White) color box**
   The text in the frame seems to disappear. When creating reverse text, the order in which you change the font color or object color doesn't matter. Regardless of the order, when you create black and white reverse text, at some point they will both be the same color. Now you can change the fill color of the text frame.

4. Click the **Fill Color button** 🖌 on the Formatting toolbar, then click the **Main (Black) color box**
   The object's background changes to black. In order to see the reversed text effect, you have to deselect the text frame.

QuickTip
Remember that when objects are selected, everything is displayed as if reversed.

5. Click outside the text frame
   Compare your work to Figure E-24. No matter how much you enhance your work with fonts, styles, and elegant designs, poor spelling will reflect poorly on any publication.

6. Press **[F9]**, spell check your publication, then click the **2-3 page icon**

7. Click the **pull quote at 15" H/6" V**, press **[F9]**, then replace the existing text with the sample shown in Figure E-25 *(substituting your name for Michael Ravenwood)*
   Even though the job isn't complete, a printout of the publication helps you evaluate your progress.

8. Click the **Save button** 🖫 on the Standard toolbar, click **File** on the menu bar, click **Print**, then print pages 1 through 3

9. Click **File** on the menu bar, then click **Exit**

FIGURE E-23: Selected text frame

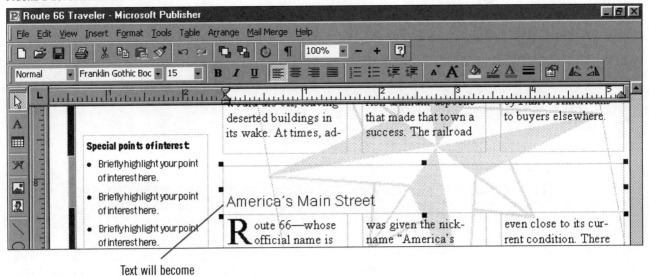

Text will become
reversed

FIGURE E-24: Reversed text in frame

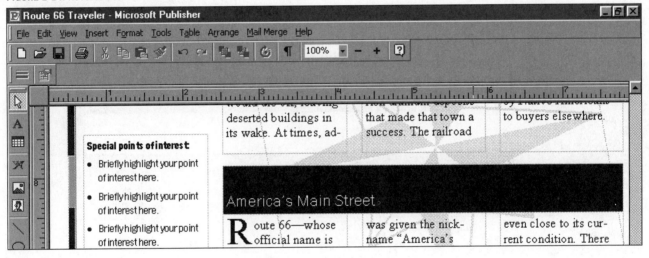

FIGURE E-25: Pull quote text

Practice

► Concepts Review

Label each of these elements in the Publisher window shown in Figure E-26.

FIGURE E-26

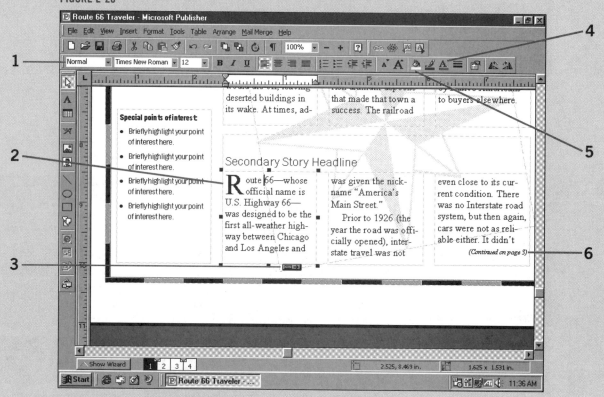

Match each of the buttons and pointers with the statement that describes its function.

7.
8.
9.
10.
11.
12.

a. Pouring pointer
b. Pitcher pointer
c. Go to Next Frame button
d. Text in overflow button
e. Go to Previous Frame button
f. Connect Text Frames button

Select the best answer from the list of choices.

13. Select the entire contents of a frame by pressing
    a. [Shift][A]
    b. [Alt][A]
    c. [Ctrl][A]
    d. [Esc][A]

14. Once you click the Connect Frame button, the pointer looks like
    a.
    b.
    c.
    d.

15. Which button takes you to the next frame?
    a.
    b.
    c.
    d.

16. Which button indicates the existence of overflow text?
    a.
    b.
    c.
    d.

17. Which dialog box is used to create Continued on/from notices?
    a. Continued Notices
    b. Notices
    c. Frame Properties
    d. Text Frame Properties

18. Changing a format into a style is called
    a. Format stylization.
    b. Creating a style by example.
    c. Stylizing a format.
    d. Creating a format master.

19. Which pointer is used to pour overflow text into a text frame?
    a.
    b.
    c.
    d.

20. **Adjusting the spaces between characters is called**
    a. Spacing.
    b. Kerning.
    c. Carning.
    d. Adjusting.

21. **Which dialog box controls the number of columns in a text frame?**
    a. Text Frame Characteristics
    b. Columns in Text Frame
    c. Modify Columns
    d. Text Frame Properties

22. **Which dialog box adds/removes a drop cap?**
    a. Drop Cap
    b. Text Frame Properties
    c. Fancy First Letter
    d. Spacing Between Characters

 # Skills Review

Throughout these exercises, use the Zoom feature where necessary. If you are using a floppy disk to save your completed publications, you need to copy the following files to another floppy disk in order to complete the Skills Review material for this unit.

1. **Define styles.**
   a. Start Publisher.
   b. Use the Catalog's Newsletters Wizard to create a newsletter for Santa Fe, NM. Select the Southwest Newsletter, accept all defaults, use the Secondary Business Personal Information set, and apply the Crocus color scheme.
   c. Save the file on your Project Disk as Santa Fe Newsletter.
   d. Hide the Wizard.
   e. Create a new text style that is 18 point Franklin Gothic Demi.
   f. Name the new style Secondary headline.
   g. Click the 2-3 page icon, then apply the Secondary headline to the Inside Story Headline at 3" H/7¾" V.
   h. Return to page 1 of the newsletter.
   i. Save your work.

2. **Modify and apply a style.**
   a. Change the font size of the Secondary headline style to 16 points.
   b. Change the effect of the Secondary headline style to Shadow.
   c. Apply the Secondary headline style to the Secondary Story Headline on page 1.
   d. Save your work.

3. **Change a format into a style.**
   a. Select the Lead Story Headline text frame on page 1.
   b. Using the Style list box, create a style called "SF Headline" that uses the formatting in the Lead Story Headline.
   c. Apply the SF Headline style to the Inside Story Headline on page 3 at 10" H/1" V.
   d. Save your work.

4. Create columns.

   a. Show the wizard while still on pages 2 and 3.

   b. Change the number of columns on the Left Inside Page to a combination column layout, then hide the wizard.

   c. Save the publication.

5. Adjust text overflows.

   a. Select the middle text frame on page 2 at 3" H/6" V, then delete the text.

   b. Select the Inside Story Headline on page 2 and change it to Santa Fe Events.

   c. Select the text frame on page 1 at 3" H/9" V, then delete the text.

   d. Select the Secondary Story Headline text on page 1 and change it to Santa Fe Events.

   e. Insert the text file PUB E-3 into the empty text frame on page 1. Do not use overflows.

   f. Using the Connect Text Frames button, pour the text into the empty text frame on page 2.

   g. Save the publication.

6. Add Continued on/from notices.

   a. Add a Continued on notice on the third column text frame in the "Santa Fe Events" story on page 1.

   b. Use the Go to Next Frame button to add a Continued from notice in the first column of the "Santa Fe Events" story on page 2.

   c. Save the publication.

7. Add drop caps.

   a. Click anywhere in the first paragraph of the Santa Fe Events story on page 1.

   b. Create a dropped custom first letter 2 lines high, using the default font.

   c. Save your work.

8. Create reversed text.

   a. Select the entire contents of the "Santa Fe Events" headline on page 1.

   b. Change the font color to Accent 2.

   c. Change the fill color to Accent 1.

   d. Save your work.

   e. Spell check all the stories in the publication.

   f. If necessary to distinguish your work from others', replace the bullets on page 1 with your name.

   g. Print pages 1 and 2 of the publication.

   h. Exit Publisher.

▶ Independent Challenges

1. A local investment company, Finance Wizardry, wants to hold monthly seminars to make people feel more comfortable with financial securities. They have hired you to create a brochure that announces these free seminars. You want to use the Catalog to create the brochure and start planning some of the brochure style elements.

To complete this independent challenge:

a. Start Publisher if necessary, use the Slant Event Brochure Catalog Wizard, accepting all defaults. Change to the Secondary Business Personal Information set.

b. Change the color scheme to Island, then hide the wizard.

c. Save the publication as Finance Wizardry Brochure on your Project Disk.

d. Create a style called "Main story" that uses a 12-point Times New Roman font and has full justification.

e. Apply the Main story style to the Main Inside Heading document (at 2" H/2" V) on page 2.

f. Add a 2-line custom drop cap for the entire Main Inside Heading story.

g. On page 1, replace the text in the frame at 9" H/1½" V with the name Finance Wizardry.

h. Create a reversed text effect in the text frame at 9" H/1½" V. Change the text to the Accent 1 color; change the background to the Main (Black) color.

i. Add your name to the e-mail address at 5" H/8" V.

j. Save and print both pages of the publication.

k. Exit Publisher.

2. To attract new homebuyers and businesses, the Chamber of Commerce has hired you to create an informative newsletter about your community. This newsletter will be sent to anyone requesting information on your community.

To complete this independent challenge:

a. Start Publisher if necessary, use the Marquee Newsletter Catalog Wizard, accepting all defaults. Change to the Secondary Business Personal Information set.

b. Change the color scheme to Lagoon, then hide the wizard.

c. Save the publication as Community Promotion Newsletter on your Project Disk.

d. Create a style by example called Story Headline based on the Lead Story Headline on page 1.

e. Apply the story headline to the Secondary Story Headline on page 1.

f. Use Word to write a 4 to 6-paragraph story about a special event in your community. Save this story as Special Event.

g. Delete the text on page 2 at 3" H/6" V.

h. Delete the text beneath the Secondary Story Headline on page 1, then insert the Special Event text file. *Do not use autoflow.*

i. Pour the overflow text on page 1 into the text frame at 3" H/6" V on page 2.

j. Add a 2-line-high drop cap to the Special Event story on page 1.

k. Add Continued on and Continued from notices on pages 1 and 2 of the Special Event story.

l. Add your name to the pull quote on page 2 at 1" H/6" V.

m. Save and print pages 1 and 2 of the publication.

n. Exit Publisher.

3. Your school wants to hold a fund-raiser for the local animal shelter. You have been hired to create this brochure and decide what type of fund-raising activity should be used.
  To complete this independent challenge:

a. Start Publisher if necessary, use the Mobile Fund-raiser Flyer Catalog Wizard, accepting all defaults. Change to the Secondary Business Personal Information set.

b. Change the color scheme to Nutmeg, then hide the wizard.

c. Save the publication as Animal Shelter Flyer on your Project Disk.

d. Decide on a title for your fund-raiser, then type it in the text frame at 2" H/2" V.

e. Create a new style called "Body text" using 14-point Times New Roman font, small caps effect, center justified.

f. Apply this style to the text frame at 5" H/5" V.

g. Make up your own text in this frame that describes the event.

h. Add your name to the e-mail address at 1" H/8½" V.

i. Save and print the publication.

j. Exit Publisher.

4. Your recent employment with the AAA Road Club is already exciting. They have asked you to design a brochure for a bus trip to see the leaves change in Maine in September, October, and November. Before you can design this brochure, you plan to use the Internet to find out more about the state of Maine.
  To complete this independent challenge:

a. Connect to the Internet and use your browser and favorite search engine to find information about the state of Maine. Find out what towns and attractions might be of interest when the leaves are changing.

b. Start Publisher if necessary, use any Informational Brochure Catalog Wizard, accepting all defaults. Change to the Secondary Business Personal Information set.

c. Change to any color scheme you choose, then hide the wizard.

d. Save the publication as Maine Leaves Brochure on your Project Disk.

e. Use the information you obtained from the Internet to write a Word 4 to 6-paragraph document about what to see and do in Maine. Name this document Maine Attractions.

f. Replace any default text.

g. Choose a location (on two pages) for the Maine Attractions document.

h. Delete any text in frames for the Maine Attractions document, then pour the story into the frames.

i. Add drop caps and continued notices.

j. Save the publication.

k. Add your name to a pull quote in the publication.

l. Print the pages in the publication containing your work.

m. Exit Publisher.

Visual Workshop

Use the Catalog to create the Linear Accent Informational Brochure (use the Informational category in the Brochure Wizards). Save this publication on your Project Disk as SW Brochure. Use Figure E-27 as a guide. Accept all the wizards' defaults, apply the Secondary Business Personal Information set, then change the color scheme to Sapphire. In the lower-right corner, substitute your name for Michael Ravenwood (in the e-mail address). Replace all text as shown in the figure, update the Personal Information (as necessary), and add the supplied images and text files. Be sure to spell check your work. Save and print page 2 of the flyer. Use PUB E-4 for the hot air balloon text, and PUB E-5 for the Canyon de Chelly text. The files Rabbit.tif, balloons.tif, canyon.tif, and spider.tif are provided for this exercise.

FIGURE E-27

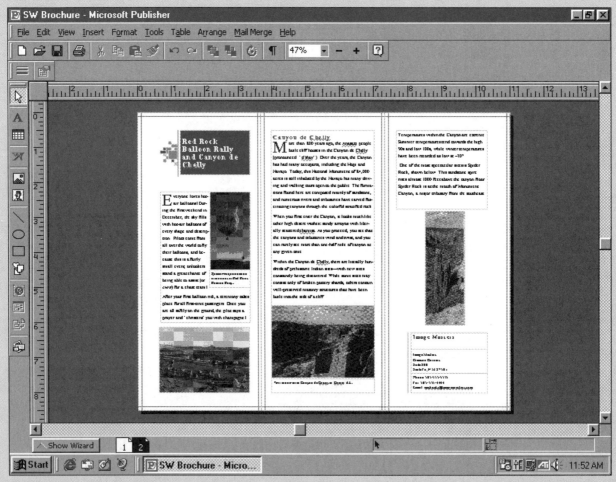

Working
with Multiple Pages

Objectives

- ▶ **Add a page**
- ▶ **Delete a page**
- ▶ **Work with a background**
- ▶ **Create a header and footer**
- ▶ **Add page numbers**
- ▶ **Edit a story**
- ▶ **Modify a table of contents**
- ▶ **Create a label**

Some publications, such as flyers, business cards, or signs, have to be designed as a single page; however, many publications have multiple pages. Publisher makes it easy to add, copy, and delete pages. For a more professional look, repetitive text, such as a title, can be displayed in the same location on the top or bottom of each page. A table of contents can be added to help readers find specific stories. Page numbers help organize the publication. ✐ Joe Gillis, an account executive at Image Masters, is designing a catalog of Native American rugs for the Navajo Nation. When finished, this catalog will be quite large and will require elements common to a multi-page document.

Publisher 2000

Adding a Page

Pages can be added to a publication one at a time. Depending on how your publication is laid out, you may want to add pages in multiples of two or four. A catalog, for example, prints pages in groups of four, so pages added in multiples of other than four can make printing cumbersome. Background items—for example, layout guides and objects such as headers and footers—are automatically added to new pages if you choose to duplicate page objects. You also have the option to copy any text or graphic objects from any page to a newly inserted page. ✐ Joe uses the Catalog to start a new publication for his project.

Steps 1 2 3 4

1. Start Publisher, click **Catalogs** in the Wizards list, click **Linear Accent Catalog**, then click **Start Wizard**

   The Flyer appears on the screen. Simple modifications can be made using the Wizard.

2. Click **Finish**, click **Personal Information** in the Catalog Wizard, click the **Secondary Business option button**, click **Update**, then, if necessary, change the entries to **Carlos Mendoza** in the Name text box, **Account Executive** in the title text box, **Image Masters, Crimson Corners, Suite 200, Santa Fe, NM, 87501** in the Address text box, **Phone: 505-555-5555, Fax: 505-555-4444, Email** *carlos.mendoza@imagemasters.com*, in the Phone/fax/e-mail text box, **Image Masters** in the Organization name text box, **We make you look your best** in the Tag line text box, then click **Update**

3. Click **Color Scheme** in the Catalogs Wizard, click **Sagebrush** in the Color Scheme list, click the **Hide Wizard button** ▼ Hide Wizard , then save the publication as **Rug Catalog** on your Project Disk

   The catalog currently contains eight pages. You can easily add any number of pages either before or after the current page. To retain a consistent design, you can also choose to duplicate objects—such as text or picture frames—from any specific page. You want to insert four new pages after page 2.

4. Click the **2-3 page icon** on the status bar, click **Insert** on the menu bar, then click **Page**

   The Insert Pages dialog box opens, as shown in Figure F-1. List arrows for the left- and right-hand pages allow you to select the type of layout on each new page. Each layout choice is consistent with your current design scheme.

5. Click **More Options**

   The Insert Page dialog box opens, as shown in Figure F-2. You can use this dialog box to control the number of new pages added as well as options such as inserting blank pages or duplicating objects on a specific page. You want to accept the default and add four pages after the current page, using the default layout and location.

QuickTip

Move a page by inserting a new page and duplicating the objects from the page you want moved, then deleting the original page.

6. Click **Cancel**, click **OK**, then click **Yes** to automatically insert four pages

   Compare your work to Figure F-3. The **4-5 page icon button** is selected on the status bar. The page icons on the status bar indicate that the publication now has 12 pages. The page icons always show you the currently displayed page and the total number of pages in the publication. Each of the newly inserted pages (4–7) has the same layout: one column, all text.

7. Click the **Save button** 🖫 on the Standard toolbar

FIGURE F-1: Insert Pages dialog box

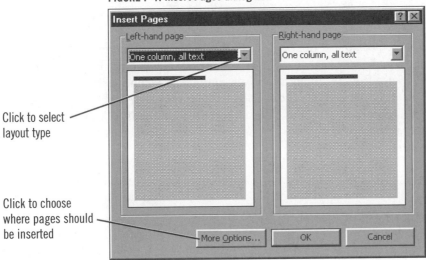

Click to select layout type

Click to choose where pages should be inserted

FIGURE F-2: Insert Page dialog box

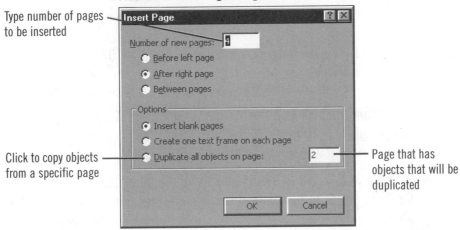

Type number of pages to be inserted

Click to copy objects from a specific page

Page that has objects that will be duplicated

FIGURE F-3: Publication with added pages

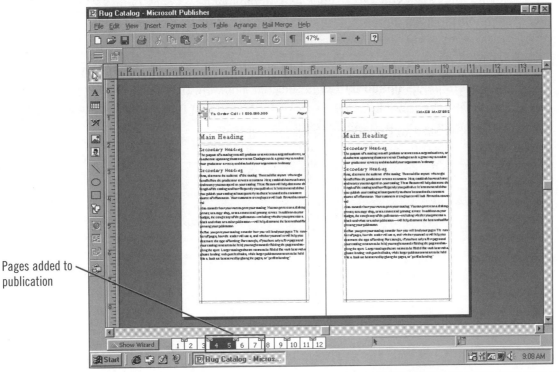

Pages added to publication

Deleting a Page

Pages that are not needed can be deleted. As a safety measure, Publisher has been designed so that you must view the page that you are deleting. When you delete a page, any objects on that page are deleted from the publication. Any continued on/continued from notices are automatically recalculated, and text in a connected frame is moved to the closest available frame on the next page. ✐ Because this project is so new, Joe wants to keep the file size small, so he eliminates any unnecessary pages. He wants to delete the four new pages as well as four additional pages.

Steps

QuickTip

If you delete a page in error, immediately click the Undo button on the Standard toolbar.

1. **Verify that pages 4-5 are displayed, click Edit on the menu bar, then click Delete Page**
   The dialog box shown in Figure F-4 opens. The Both pages option button is selected, although you could just delete the left or right page. Since you know that a catalog adds and deletes an even number of pages, you want to see what happens if you try to delete a single page.

2. **Click the Left page only option button, then click OK**
   The warning dialog box shown in Figure F-5 opens. This tells you that you can delete a single page, but your layout may be adversely affected or you can cancel this operation.

3. **Click Cancel, click Edit on the menu bar, click Delete Page, verify that the Both pages option button is selected, click OK, then click OK**
   You can see that your publication now has 10 pages: two pages fewer than before.

4. **With pages 4-5 still active, click Edit on the menu bar, click Delete Page, verify that the Both pages option button is selected, then click OK**
   There are now eight pages in the publication. You can delete more pages from this publication.

5. **With pages 4-5 still active, click Edit on the menu bar, click Delete Page, verify that the Both pages option button is selected, click OK, then click OK**
   There are now six pages in the catalog.

6. **With pages 4-5 still active, click Edit on the menu bar, click Delete Page, verify that the Both pages option button is selected, click OK, then click the page 2-3 icon**
   Compare your catalog to Figure F-6. There are now four pages in the publication.

7. **Click the Save button 🖫 on the Standard toolbar**

FIGURE F-4: Delete Page dialog box

FIGURE F-5: Multiple pages warning dialog box

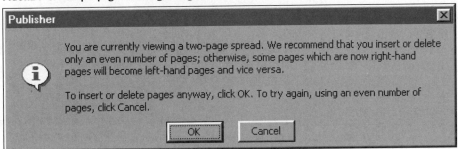

FIGURE F-6: Two-page spread

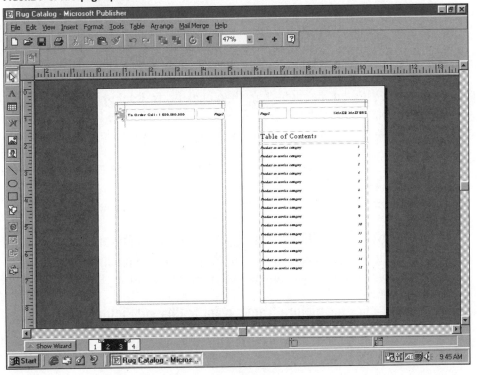

Saving objects on a page

When a page is deleted, all the objects on that page are also deleted. What if you want to save some of those objects for later use? Any objects can be pulled onto the **scratch area**, the gray area surrounding the page in the workspace. Objects in the scratch area are saved along with the publication and can be viewed and accessed from all pages in the publication. When you've decided where you want an object from the scratch area to be used, move it to its new location using any copying/pasting technique.

Working with a Background

Every publication has a page background that can be used to add text or objects that you want on every page. A publication without mirrored guides has a single background page, while a publication with mirrored guides has both left and right backgrounds. You can use the background to add an object, such as a logo, to each page or to only one page. Joe wants descriptive text about Navajo rugs on page 2. Once he inserts this text, he adds an image of a rug to the background page.

Steps

1. Click the **Text Frame Tool button** A on the Objects toolbar, then drag the + pointer from **1" H/2" V to 4½" H/7¼" V**

   The text frame appears on the page. You can insert prepared text in the frame.

2. Right-click the **text frame**, point to **Change Text**, click **Text File**, locate **PUB F-1** on your Project Disk, then click **OK**

   All the text fits within the frame, as shown in Figure F-7. In order for background objects behind the text frame to be visible, the text frame fill must be eliminated.

3. Right-click the **text frame**, point to **Change Frame**, point to **Fill Color**, then click **No Fill**

   When a background is in place, the clear text frame allows any objects to be visible.

QuickTip

Modify an existing background by switching to the background view and editing objects.

4. Click **View** on the menu bar, then click **Go to Background**

   The blank mirrored background pages appear. Background pages can accommodate both text and graphics. The catalog will look very elegant with recolored rug images in the background.

5. Click the **Picture Frame Tool button** 🖻 on the Objects toolbar, drag the + pointer from **1" H/2" V to 4½" H/6½" V**

   The picture frame is in place on the left background page.

6. Right-click the **picture frame**, point to **Change Picture**, point to **Picture**, click **From File**, locate **Wruins-1.tif** on your Project Disk, then click **Insert**

   The picture is inserted into the picture frame. Recoloring the picture will give it a nice effect.

QuickTip

The ScreenTip displays the color name on the Scheme colors palette.

7. Right-click the **picture frame**, point to **Change Picture**, click **Recolor Picture**, click the **Color list arrow**, click **Accent 4 Scheme color**, then click **OK**

   The rug image has a gray appearance, as shown in Figure F-8.

QuickTip

You can toggle between the foreground and background views using the [Ctrl][M] shortcut keys.

8. Click **View** on the menu bar, then click **Go to Foreground**

   The recolored image appears behind the text in the frame. Compare your work to Figure F-9.

9. Click the **Save button** 🖫 on the Standard toolbar

FIGURE F-7: Text file added to publication

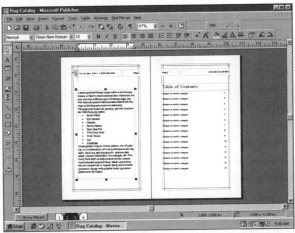

FIGURE F-8: Recolored image added to background

Image on left
background page

Left background
pages will have
even numbers

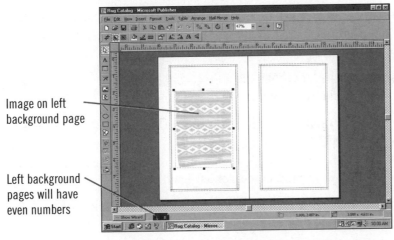

FIGURE F-9: Text in foreground, image in background

Having no fill
color in text
file makes
background
visible

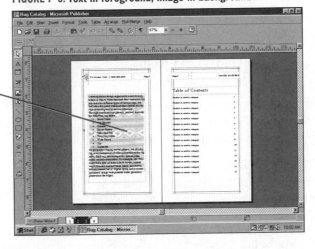

Changing from double to single background pages

If you have mirrored layout guides, you also have left and right background pages. You can easily change from double to single background pages by deselecting the Create Two Backgrounds with Mirrored Guides check box in the Layout Guides dialog box. When this check box is not selected, you have only one background page. What was previously the right background page is now used as the publication's background page and is applied to all the pages.

Creating a Header and Footer

Text that repeats on the top of each page is called a **header**, and text that repeats on the bottom of each page is a **footer**. In most cases, headers and footers are added to the background of pages. You have the option of ignoring the background on any page in the publication so you can choose which pages headers and footers. You create a text frame for the header or footer text and position it on the right or left background page. Images can also be included in headers or footers to enhance the publication. ✒ The Catalog automatically added several text frames in the foreground, which Joe decides are unnecessary and would like to delete. Joe wants to add a header containing a descriptive name for this publication to the background of the catalog

Steps

1. Click the **frame** at 4" H/1" V, press and hold **[Shift]**, click the **frame** at 7" H/1" V, click the **frame** at 9" H/1" V, press **[Delete]**, then release **[Shift]**
   The text frames are deleted from the publication.

2. Click **View** on the menu bar, click **Go to Background**
   There are no text boxes visible in the background.

   > **QuickTip**
   > Use the guidelines to define the frame.

3. Click the **Text Frame Tool button** [A] on the Objects toolbar, drag the + pointer from 2¾" H/½" V to 4¾" H/¾" V, then press **[F9]**
   You added a text frame at the top-right corner of the left background page. This text frame will contain the descriptive header for left-hand pages.

4. Type **Navajo Rugs: A Living History**, then click the **Align Right button** [≡] on the Formatting toolbar
   Compare your page to Figure F-10. The quick copy feature can duplicate this text frame and place it directly across on the right background page aligned horizontally with the original.

   > **QuickTip**
   > Use the scroll bars to reposition the screen so that you can see the text frames in both left and right background pages.

5. Position the ⬒ pointer over the **left background page text frame**, press and hold **[Ctrl]**, press and hold **[Shift]**, press the **left mouse button**, when the pointer changes to ⬚, drag the **copy of the frame** so the left edge of the copy is at 6¼" H, aligned with the blue layout guide and the top edge is aligned with the pink layout guide, release the left mouse button, release **[Ctrl]**, release **[Shift]**, then click the **Align Left button** [≡] on the Formatting toolbar
   Compare your headers to Figure F-11.

6. Press **[F9]**, click **View** on the menu bar, click **Go to Foreground**
   The header is displayed on pages 2 and 3, as shown in Figure F-12. Catalogs typically don't have headers on page 1.

7. Click the **page 1 icon** on the status bar
   Currently, the header is partially hidden behind the pull quote.

8. Click **View** on the menu bar, then click **Ignore Background**
   Because you chose to ignore the background on this first page, any objects on the right background page are not visible on this page.

9. Click the **Save button** [💾] on the Standard toolbar

FIGURE F-10: Text frame for left background page header

Header text frame in left background page

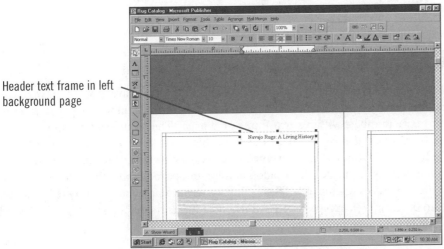

Navajo Rugs: A Living History

FIGURE F-11: Headers on left and right background pages

Right header

Left header

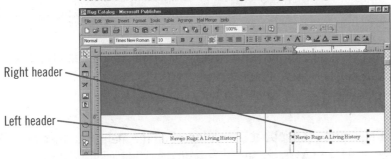

Navajo Rugs: A Living History   Navajo Rugs: A Living History

FIGURE F-12: Headers visible on left and right pages

Headers on background pages

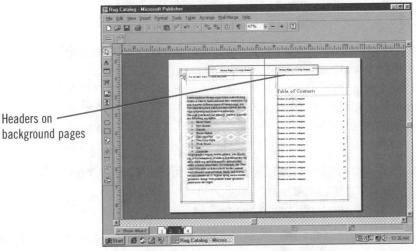

Masking background objects

Ignoring background elements is a good way to eliminate all background objects for a particular page. If, however, you want to ignore some—but not all—background objects, using the Ignore Background command won't work. You can block out specific background elements by creating a mask in the foreground. Create a mask by clicking the Text Frame Tool button on the Objects toolbar, changing the fill color to mask the object, and dragging the outline over the background element(s) you want to hide. With this method, the background elements are preserved, and each page in a publication has exactly the look you want.

Publisher 2000

Adding Page Numbers

You will probably want to add page numbers to publications that have more than two pages. Page numbers make it easy for readers to find stories that are continued on several pages. You can manually insert page numbers within a text frame on a page. The pound sign symbol (#) automatically inserts the calculated correct page number. This is the same way that Publisher calculates page numbers for Continued on/Continued from notices. As pages are added and deleted, your page numbers remain accurate. Like headers and footers, page numbers are added in background pages so they appear on each page. Joe wants automatic page numbers in the footers at the bottom of each page, except page 1 (which already has the background ignored). He begins by changing to the background view.

Steps

1. Click **View** on the menu bar, then click **Go to Background**
   The background facing pages are displayed. You want the page numbers to appear in the bottom-right corner of the left background page and the bottom-left corner of the right background page.

2. Click the **Text Frame Tool button** 🅰 on the Objects toolbar, drag the + pointer from **¾" H/7¾" V** to **1½" H/8" V**, then press **[F9]**
   The text frame is in place on the left background page for the automatic page number for left-hand pages in the publication.

3. Type **Page**, press **[Spacebar]**, click **Insert** on the menu bar, then click **Page Numbers**
   You can copy this text frame and place it on the right background page, just as you did with the descriptive header.

4. Click the **Zoom Out button** ⊟ on the Standard toolbar, then use the horizontal scroll bar to position the pages as shown in Figure F-13
   You can see both the left and right edges of the pages.

5. Press and hold **[Ctrl]**, press and hold **[Shift]**, position the pointer over the text frame, press the **left mouse button**, when the pointer changes to 🖱, drag the **copy of the text frame** so the right edge of the text frame is at **10¼" H**, release the left mouse button, release **[Shift]**, then release **[Ctrl]**
   A copy of the text frame with the page number is placed on the right background page. In order to be consistent, the text in the right footer can be right-aligned.

6. Click the **Align Right button** ▤ on the Formatting toolbar, press **[Ctrl][M]**, then click the **Page 2-3 page icon**
   Compare your page footers with Figure F-14.

7. Click the **Zoom list arrow** 36% ▾ on the Standard toolbar, then click **Whole Page**
   Pages 2 and 3 are displayed full screen, as shown in Figure F-15.

8. Click the **Save button** 🖫 on the Standard toolbar

FIGURE F-13: Background pages positioned on screen

Footer text frame

FIGURE F-14: Page numbers are displayed from background

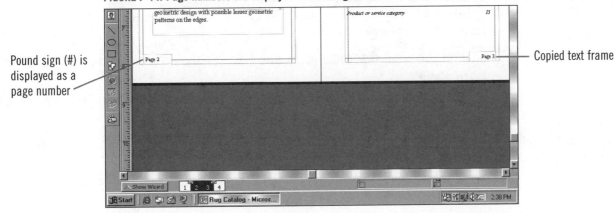

Pound sign (#) is displayed as a page number

Copied text frame

FIGURE F-15: Resulting pages

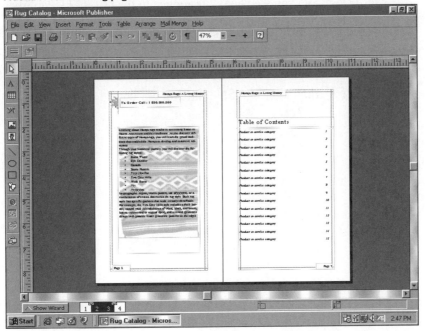

Editing a Story

Text in a publication—called a **story**—can be typed directly into a text frame or prepared beforehand and inserted as a text file. In some cases, you might want to edit a story while working in Publisher. If a version of Microsoft Word 6.0 or later is installed on your computer, you can edit the story directly in Word. Editing directly in Word lets you take advantage of Word's features from within Publisher. ✎✎✎ After reading the publication, Joe wants to make changes to the descriptive text on page 2.

Steps

1. Click the text frame at 3" H/3" V, then press [F9]

The text frame is zoomed to 100% on your screen. You can edit the story in this frame using Word.

Trouble?

If Word isn't installed on your computer, edit the story directly in Publisher. If you edit the story in Publisher, skip Step 2 and Step 5.

2. Right-click the text frame, point to Change Text, click Edit Story in Microsoft Word, then click the Maximize button in the upper-right corner of the Document in Rug Catalog window (if necessary)

Microsoft Word opens, displaying the story's text, as shown in Figure F-16. Any edits you make to this text in Word will be applied to the text in the text frame in Publisher.

3. Click anywhere in discover, press and hold [Shift], click anywhere in of, then type learn about

You changed the phrase "discover different types of " to "learn about" in the first paragraph to make the style more succinct.

QuickTip

Some text formatting, such as drop caps, is lost when moving from Word to Publisher.

4. Click to the right of Yei (the eighth bullet), press [Spacebar], type and, press [Spacebar], then press [Delete] three times

You combined two of the bulleted items into one bullet. When your edits are complete, you can exit Word and return to the story in Publisher.

5. Click File on the menu bar, then click Exit

Word closes and you see your edits applied to the text in the Publisher story.

6. Click anywhere within the first paragraph, click Format on the menu bar, click Drop Cap, click the drop cap directly under the current selection, then click OK

The drop cap is added to make the story stand out. Compare your work to Figure F-17.

7. Press [F9], then click the Save button 🖫 on the Standard toolbar

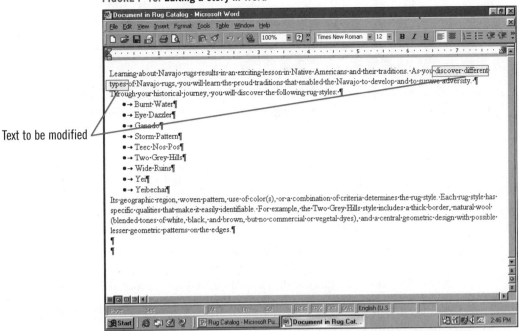

Text to be modified

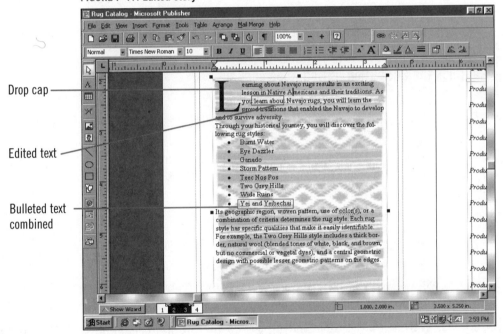

Drop cap

Edited text

Bulleted text combined

Copyfitting text

As you create a publication—particularly a newsletter—you may find that you have either too much or too little text. **Copyfitting** is a term used to describe the process of making the text fit the space within a publication. If you have too much text, you can make the margins narrower, decrease the point size of the font, increase the text frame, flow text into a frame on another page, or delete some text through editing. Solve the problem of too little text by inserting a graphic image or pull quote, making margins wider, increasing the point size of the font, or adding text. Once a text frame is selected, it can be copyfitted using the right mouse button.

Publisher 2000

Modifying a Table of Contents

A **tab**, or tab stop, is a defined location to which the insertion point advances when you press [Tab]. A **table of contents** uses tabs to align columnar information and helps readers locate the page numbers of specific stories within a publication. You make a table of contents by typing text into a text frame, and then adding tabs and dot leaders to connect the text and page number. **Dot leaders** are a series of dots that leads up to a tab. ✎ Joe wants to modify the table of contents automatically created by the Catalog. He adds dot leaders to make reading easier. Although he still has a lot of work to do, he'll also make entries to approximate where information will be found in his catalog.

Steps 1 2 3 4

1. **Click the text frame at 8" H/2" V, then press [F9]**
   The first item in the Table of Contents is for page 1. The reference to this page is not necessary. Rather than adjust each of the subsequent entries, you simply delete this line.

2. **Click to the left of the first line (Product or service category), press and hold [Shift], press [End], release [Shift], then press [Delete]**
   The first line is deleted, and the second line begins with page 2.

3. **Right-click the text frame, point to Change Text, click Highlight Entire Story, click Format on the menu bar, then click Tabs**
   The Tabs dialog box opens, as shown in Figure F-18. You want each tab to be preceded by a dot leader.

4. **Click the Dot option button, then click OK**
   Each of the entries in the text frame has a dot leader preceding the page number.

5. **Click Product or service category in the first line in the frame, type Introduction to Navajo Rugs, then press [Tab]**
   The dots begin at the end of the text and continue to the position of the tab. The first entry in the Table of Contents is complete. When you pressed [Tab], the dot leader was placed before the page number.

6. **Delete the entry for page 3, then delete the entries for pages 12–15**

7. **Type the Table of Contents information shown in Figure F-19 for the remaining rug types, using the techniques described in Step 5**
   The Table of Contents will help clients locate information about the rugs they want to read about when the catalog is complete.

8. **Press [F9], click the Save button 🖫 on the Standard toolbar, then click the Print button 🖨**
   Review the four printed pages of the catalog.

9. **Click File on the menu bar, then click Close**
   The publication is closed and Publisher is still open and available for additional work.

> **QuickTip**
> Use your own name in a final entry to the Table of Contents to distinguish your publication from others.

FIGURE F-18: Tabs dialog box

Alignment options

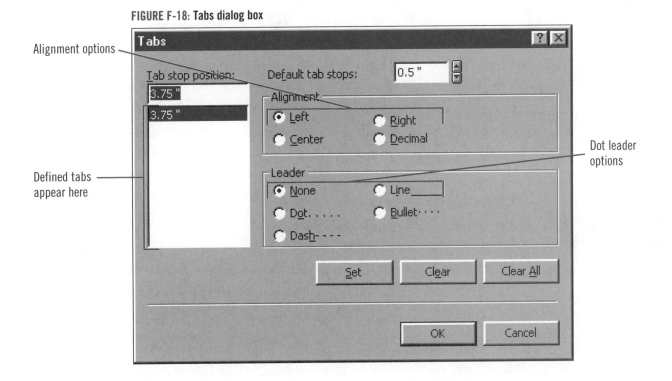

Defined tabs
appear here

Dot leader
options

FIGURE F-19: Completed Table of Contents

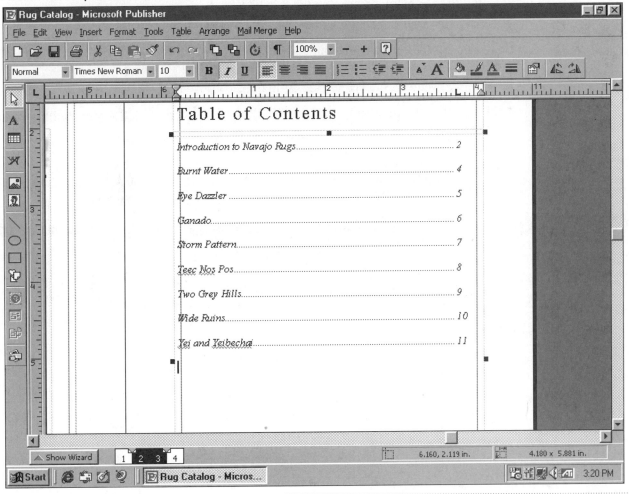

Publisher 2000

Publisher 2000

Creating a Label

You can use the Catalog to create professional-looking labels for a variety of items, such as retail products, CDs, or notebooks. These labels are designed to print directly on commercially available labels in a wide range of sizes and styles. ◄━━━━ Joe uses the Catalog to create a label that can be attached to each rug.

Steps 1234

1. Click **File** on the menu bar, click **New**, click **Labels** in the Wizards list, click **Identification**, click **Made By Tag**, click **Start Wizard,** then click **Finish**
   The label appears on the screen. It is ready to print on Avery label #5160. Simple modifications can be made using the Wizard.

2. Click **Color Scheme** in the Label Wizard, click **Sagebrush**, click **Personal Information**, click the **Secondary Business option button**, click the **Hide Wizard button** ▼ Hide Wizard , then save the publication as **Rug Label** on your Project Disk
   Any publication, even a label, has a foreground and background.

3. Press **[Ctrl][M]**, click the **Picture Frame Tool button** 🖼 on the Objects toolbar, then drag the ✛ pointer from ⅝" H/¼" V to 2" H/¾" V
   You decide that an image of a rug would be a nice addition to the label.

4. Right-click the **picture frame**, point to **Change Picture**, point to **Picture**, click **From File**, locate **Wruins-2.tif** on your Project Disk, then click **Insert**
   Compare your label to Figure F-20. As in the catalog, you can recolor the image.

5. Right-click the **picture frame**, point to **Change Picture**, click **Recolor Picture**, click the **Color list arrow**, click **Accent 4**, then click **OK**
   The image is recolored to a light gray shade.

6. Press **[Ctrl][M]**, select the text **Made especially for you by:**, type **Authentic Navajo Rug made by:**, click the **Fill Color button** 🎨 on the Formatting toolbar, then click **No Fill**

QuickTip

Use your own name in this label to distinguish your label from others.

7. Select the text **Carlos Mendoza**, type **Rose Manygoats**, click the **Fill Color button** 🎨 on the Formatting toolbar, then click **No Fill**
   Compare your label to Figure F-21.

8. Click the Save button 💾, then click the **Print button** 🖨 on the Standard toolbar, then exit Publisher

FIGURE F-20: Label with image in background

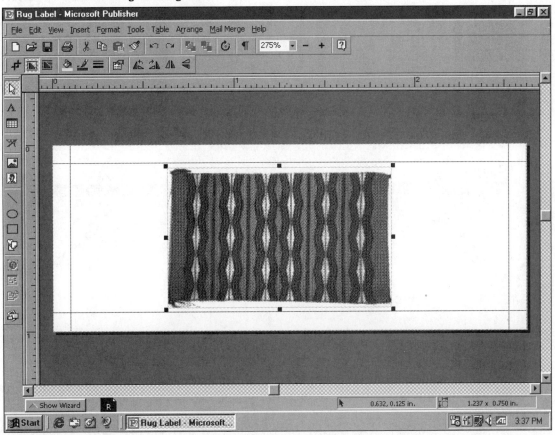

FIGURE F-21: Completed label with recolored image

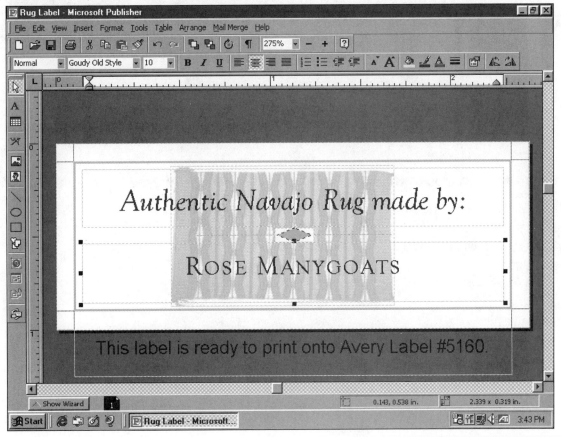

Publisher 2000

Practice

► Concepts Review

Label each of the elements of the Publisher window shown in Figure F-22.

FIGURE F-22

Match each of the features with the button, menu, or command used to perform the function.

6. Changes between background and foreground

7. Text that repeats on the bottom of each page

8. Text that repeats at the top of each page

9. Deletes a page

10. Adds dot leaders

11. Adds a drop cap

a. Footer
b. Format menu
c. Header
d. View menu
e. Tabs dialog box
f. Edit menu

Select the best answer from the list of choices.

12. The gray area surrounding the page that can be used to save objects is called the
    a. Trash area.
    b. Recycling area.
    c. Scratch area.
    d. Surplus area.

13. Each of the following is true about adding a page, *except*:
    a. Pages can be added before or after the current page.
    b. You can only add one page at a time.
    c. Existing layout guides are added to the new page(s).
    d. You can duplicate objects found on other pages in the publication.

14. Which menu is used to ignore an entire page background?
    a. Edit
    b. View
    c. Format
    d. Arrange

15. Which command is used to toggle between background and foreground pages?
    a. [Ctrl][M]
    b. [Ctrl][Y]
    c. [Ctrl][N]
    d. [Ctrl][B]

16. Where in a publication are headers and footers usually placed?
    a. Scratch area
    b. Picture frame
    c. In a central location
    d. Background

17. Which menu is used to add page numbers to a publication?
    a. Edit
    b. Insert
    c. Format
    d. Tools

18. Text that appears at the bottom of every page is called a
    a. Header.
    b. Style.
    c. Repeater.
    d. Footer.

19. Open the tabs dialog box by
    a. Using a command on the Format menu.
    b. Double-clicking a location on the horizontal ruler.
    c. Double-clicking a location on the vertical ruler.
    d. Using a command on the Table menu.

20. Which character creates automatic page numbers?
    a. @
    b. #
    c. !
    d. &

► Skills Review

Throughout these exercises, use the Zoom feature where necessary. If you are using a floppy disk to save your completed publications, you need to copy the following files to another floppy disk in order to complete the end-of-unit material for this unit.

1. Add a page

a. Start Publisher.
b. Use the Catalog to create a catalog for a video store. Select the Marquee Catalog, accept all the wizard defaults, use the Secondary Personal Information set, and apply the Nutmeg color scheme.
c. Save the file on your Project Disk as Video Store Catalog.
d. Display pages 2-3 in foreground view.
e. Insert four pages (each having the 2 columns, text and pictures layout) after page 3. You should have 12 pages in the Video Store catalog.
f. Save your work.

2. Delete a page.

a. Display pages 6 and 7.
b. Delete pages 8 through 11 (in two steps, delete pages 10 and 11, and then pages 8 and 9.)
c. Display pages 4 and 5.
d. Delete pages 6 and 7, and then delete pages 4 and 5.
e. Save your work.

3. Work with a background.

a. Change to background view.
b. Use the Clip Gallery Tool button to create a frame from 1½" H/2½" V to 4" H/6" V on page 2.
c. Search the Clip Gallery on the key words "motion pictures."
d. Select the image EN00500_.WMF (right-click the image, then click Clip Properties to verify the filename).
e. Click the image, click the Insert clip button, then close the Clip Gallery.
f. Recolor the image using the Accent 3 color.
g. Save your work.

4. Create a header and footer.

a. Draw a text frame from 3½" H/½" V to 4¾" H/¾" V on the left background page.
b. Type "Classic Videos".
c. Right-justify the text in the frame, then make the text bold.
d. Copy this text frame so that its left edge is at 6¼" H on the right background page and it aligns with the top edge of the text frame on the left page.
e. Left-justify the text in this frame.
f. Save the publication.

5. Add page numbers.

a. Create a text frame from ¾" H/7¾" V to 1¼" H/8" V on the left background page.
b. Type "Page", then press [Spacebar].
c. Use the Insert menu to add a page number.
d. Copy this text frame to the left background page so that its right edge is at 10¼" H.

e. Return to foreground view.

f. Delete the objects at the top of the left and right foreground pages.

g. Save the publication.

6. **Edit a story.**
   a. Use the Text Frame Tool button to draw a frame at 1¼" H/2½" V to 4¼" H/6½" V.
   b. Insert the text file PUB F-2 into the frame.
   c. Open Word to edit the story.
   d. Add the following text as a new paragraph at the end of the story: "If we don't have what you're looking for, we can get it for you."
   e. Exit Word.
   f. Verify that the text has been added to the story.
   g. Add a custom drop cap (a 3-line-high character using the style immediately below the current selection) to the first paragraph.
   h. Change the fill color of the text frame to No Fill.
   i. Save the publication.

7. **Modify a table of contents.**
   a. Delete the entries in the Table of Contents on page 3 for pages 1–3.
   b. Change the tab setting for the remaining entries to dot leaders.
   c. Change the remaining entries, using Table F-1 below.
   d. If necessary, add a final entry in the Table of Contents that contains your name.
   e. Save and print your work.
   f. Close the publication, but do not exit Publisher.

8. **Create a label.**
   a. Click File on the menu bar, click New, then use the Catalog to create a Video Face Label using the Label Wizard.
   b. Accept all defaults, use the Secondary Business Personal Information set, change the color scheme to Island, then save the label as Video Label on your Project Disk.
   c. Change the Video Title text to "Sunset Boulevard".
   d. Change the date text to the current date.
   e. Change the Image Masters text to your name.
   f. Save your work.
   g. Print the publication.
   h. Exit Publisher.

TABLE F-1

Blockbusters	4
1930s	6
1940s	8
1950s	10
1960s	12
Independent Films	14

Publisher 2000

▶ Independent Challenges

1. As a member of a small theater group, you understand teamwork. As the only one proficient in desktop publishing, you've been asked to create the program for the next production.

To complete this independent challenge:

a. Start Publisher, use the Programs Wizard, select the Theater Program Wizard.

b. Accept all the defaults.

c. Change to the Secondary Business Personal Information set, then hide the wizard.

d. Save the publication as Play Program on your Project Disk.

e. Switch to the background view, then add a header with the name of the play. (Choose any play with which you are familiar, such as *The Sound of Music*, *A Chorus Line*, or *Man of La Mancha*.)

f. Create a footer containing page numbers in the background. (If necessary, move any information so that your header/footer fits correctly.)

g. Add any appropriate clip art to the background, recoloring the clip art if necessary.

h. Return to the foreground, then replace any placeholders with your own text.

i. Make sure the page number and header/footer do not appear on the first page.

j. Delete the table containing the cast (on page 2) and create a text frame that will contain the names of cast members. Use friends and family members for cast members.

k. Use Word to create and edit a paragraph describing the play in the existing frame on page 3.

l. Add your name as the director. Change any text for the Acts.

m. Save the publication.

n. Check the spelling in the publication.

o. Print the publication.

p. Exit Publisher.

2. Now that you know how to use Publisher's Label Wizard, you've decided to create a shipping label you can use when you send items to other people.

To complete this independent challenge:

a. Start Publisher, select the Labels Wizards, click Shipping, then select the Borders Shipping Label (Avery 5164) Wizard, accepting all defaults.

b. Change to the Secondary Personal Information set, change to any color scheme you choose, then hide the wizard.

c. Save the publication as Personal Shipping Label on your Project Disk.

d. Edit the return address information (at 1"H/1" V) using your own name and address.

e. Insert and recolor clip art in the background view.

f. Save and print the publication.

g. Exit Publisher.

3. A local elementary school has hired you to produce a newsletter for its staff and students. You can use the Catalog to create this newsletter.

To complete this independent challenge:

a. Start Publisher, select Newsletters, select the Kid Stuff Newsletter Wizard, accepting all defaults.

b. Change to the Secondary Business Personal Information set.

c. Change the color scheme to Orchid, then hide the wizard.

d. Save the publication as School Newsletter on your Project Disk.

e. Display pages 2 and 3.

f. Open the Insert Pages dialog box. Click the left-hand page list arrow, click Calendar. Click the Right-hand page list arrow, click Response Form, then click OK.

g. Page numbers, the newsletter title, and issue information currently exist as footers in the publication. Cut the text frames from the foreground of pages 2 and 3, then paste them in the page background. (Delete the footers on the foreground of page 3.)

h. Make sure the page number—or header/footer—does not appear on the first page.

i. Make up your own headings to replace the existing placeholders.

j. Replace at least one story with your own original story.

k. Replace the newsletter title with your own school's name.

l. Edit the story in Word if you have this program available to you; otherwise, edit in Publisher.

m. Check the spelling in the publication.

n. Add your name in the Table of Contents on the first page of the newsletter.

o. Save the publication.

p. Print the publication.

q. Exit Publisher.

4. Your ability to use Publisher has become noticed by your employer, and they have asked you to teach a one-day course on how to use this program. As part of your duties, you will also have to prepare course materials on this program.
To complete this independent challenge:

a. Connect to the Internet and use your browser to go to http://www.microsoft.com. From there, click the links for Publisher 2000.

b. Find information about Publisher's highlights and capabilities, and print out any necessary information.

c. Start Publisher if necessary, use a Newsletter Catalog Wizard of your choice, accepting all defaults. Change to the Secondary Business Personal Information set.

d. Change to any color scheme you choose, then hide the wizard.

e. Save the publication as Publisher Newsletter on your Project Disk.

f. Delete some of the pages so that only two pages remain.

g. Create a title for your newsletter, and create a lead and secondary story. Edit the stories in Word, if possible. (Use information from the Publisher Web site in the stories.)

h. Add any clip art you feel is appropriate.

i. Delete the existing Table of Contents frame on page 1, and then create a text frame in the same location for the Table of Contents.

j. Be sure to use dot leaders in the Table of Contents, and add your name to the first entry in the Table of Contents.

k. Check the spelling in the publication.

l. Save and print the publication.

m. Exit Publisher.

▶ Visual Workshop

Use the Catalog to create the Binder label (use the Labels category in the Catalog). Save this publication on your Project Disk as Rug Collection Binder. Use Figure F-23 as a guide. Accept the Wizard defaults, apply the Secondary Business Personal Information set, then delete page 2. At the bottom of page 1, substitute your name. Replace all text as shown in the figure, and add the image Yeirug.tif, which is provided on your Project Disk, to the background. Save and print the page.

FIGURE F-23

Using
Special Features

Objectives

▶ **Add BorderArt**
▶ **Create an object shadow**
▶ **Design WordArt**
▶ **Create a watermark**
▶ **Wrap text around a frame**
▶ **Rotate a text frame**
▶ **Prepare for commercial printing**
▶ **Use the Pack and Go Wizard**

Now that you know how to use Publisher to create a publication, you're ready to explore the special features that add interesting elements to your work and add effects found in professionally created publications. Publisher's special features are fun and easy to use. You can add fancy borders to frames, create curved text designs, wrap text around a frame, rotate text frames, and make your work portable. ✎ Marnie Roberts is an account representative for Piano Magic, a new Image Masters' client specializing in the sale and service of pianos. Marnie is working on designing the first page of an informational brochure.

Publisher 2000

Adding BorderArt

Attractive borders can add pizzazz to a publication. Borders can be added to any frame. As with any design element, judicious use creates a professional look. Rather than spending a lot of time creating these borders, users can take advantage of **BorderArt**, fancy decorative borders that come with Publisher. A fancy border is added to a frame using a tab in the BorderArt dialog box. Marnie wants to add an eye-catching border design to the first page of the brochure.

Steps 1234

1. Start Publisher, click **Brochures** in the Wizards list, click **Informational**, click the **Frames Informational Brochure**, click **Start Wizard**, then click **Finish**
   The Wizard creates a two-page informational brochure.

2. Click **Personal Information** in the Brochure Wizard, click the **Secondary Business option button**, click **Update**, then, if necessary, change the entries to **Carlos Mendoza** in the Name text box, **Account Executive** in the title text box, **Image Masters, Crimson Corners, Suite 200, Santa Fe, NM, 87501** in the Address text box, **Phone: 505-555-5555, Fax: 505-555-4444, Email** carlos.mendoza@imagemasters.com, in the Phone/fax/e-mail text box, **Image Masters** in the Organization name text box, **We make you look your best.** in the Tag line text box, then click **Update**

3. Click **Color Scheme** in the Catalog Wizard, click **Clay** in the Color Scheme list, click **Hide Wizard**, then save the publication as **Piano Magic Brochure** on your Project Disk
   To enhance the front of the brochure, you can add a fancy border.

QuickTip

Before clicking the frame, use the ScreenTip to verify that you're selecting the rectangle rather than a text frame.

4. Click the **rectangle at 8" H/6" V**
   Compare your screen to Figure G-1. Once a frame or object is selected, you can modify its border.

5. Right-click the **rectangle**, point to **Change Rectangle**, point to **Line/Border Style**, then click **More Styles**
   The Border Style dialog box opens. Borders can be simple lines of varying thickness or color, or they can be fanciful images. You want a border that suggests a musical theme.

6. Click the **BorderArt tab**, scroll through the **list of Available Borders**, then click **Music Notes**
   Figure G-2 shows the BorderArt tab with the Music Notes border selected. Available borders are listed in alphabetical order. When you click a border, the sample is displayed around the perimeter of the Preview box. You can change the size of the individual images in BorderArt to modify the border's appearance.

QuickTip

Remove existing BorderArt from a frame by opening the Border Style dialog box, selecting None (the first option in the list of Available Borders), then clicking OK.

7. Double-click **16** in the Border size text box, type **12**, click **OK**, then press **[F9]**
   The BorderArt pattern appears on the edge of the rectangle, as shown in Figure G-3. Now that the BorderArt is added to the object, you are beginning to create a brochure that has the style you are looking for.

8. Press **[F9]**, then click the **Save button** 🖫 on the Standard toolbar

FIGURE G-1: Object selected

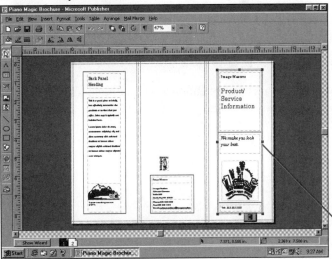

BorderArt will be
applied to rectangle

FIGURE G-2: Border Style dialog box

Available borders
appear here

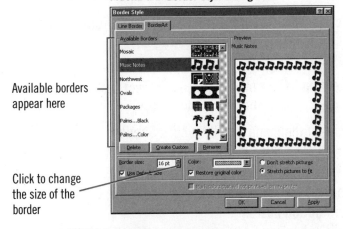

Click to change
the size of the
border

FIGURE G-3: BorderArt added to object

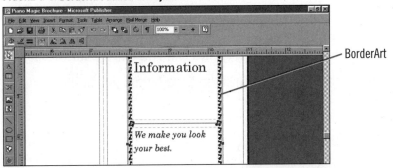

BorderArt

Create custom BorderArt

Almost any simple clip art or graphic image can
be turned into BorderArt. Once the BorderArt tab
in the Border Style dialog box is selected, click
Create Custom. You can choose from images in
the Clip Gallery or elsewhere on your computer.
You can even create BorderArt from images you
created yourself. Click the Choose Picture button,
locate the image, click OK, choose a name for
your border, then click OK. Figure G-4 shows a
custom border created from the Clip Gallery.

FIGURE G-4: Custom border in Border Style dialog box

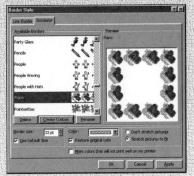

Creating an Object Shadow

There are many ways to call attention to a frame besides formatting its contents. You can, for example, add or delete an object shadow using the Formatting toolbar. Shadows add the illusion of depth. When applied, an object shadow appears behind the currently selected frame. Marnie wants to replace a placeholder object located within the border art and add a shadow behind the image to give it a 3-D effect.

Steps

1. **Click the picture frame object at 9" H/6" V, then press [F9]**
   The object is enlarged. You decide to replace the object with an image more appropriate to the theme of pianos for the brochure. Piano Magic supplied an image in the form of a .wmf file.

2. **Right-click the selected object, point to Change Picture, point to Picture, then click From File**
   The Insert Picture dialog box opens.

3. **Click the Look in list arrow, locate your Project Disk, click piano, then click Insert**
   The piano image replaces the placeholder image.

4. **Click Format on the menu bar, then click Shadow**
   The shadow appears behind the frame, as shown in Figure G-5. You can change the fill color inside the frame.

5. **Click Format on the menu bar, point to Fill Color, click More Colors, then click the Basic colors option button**
   The Colors dialog box opens, as shown in Figure G-6. You choose a color to enhance the image.

QuickTip

You can see how a color looks before closing the Colors dialog box by clicking Apply. You may have to relocate the dialog box so you can see the applied color.

6. **Click the Sky blue color box in column 10 in the Blue row, click OK, then click the scratch area**
   The sky blue color is applied to fill the object frame, as shown in Figure G-7.

7. **Press [F9], then click the Save button 💾 on the Standard toolbar**

FIGURE G-5: Enlarged object with shadow

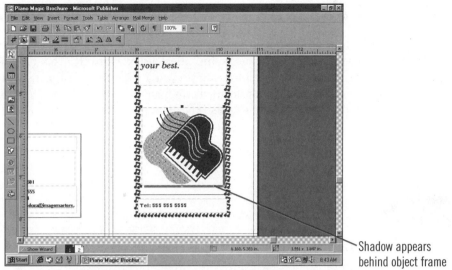

Shadow appears
behind object frame

FIGURE G-6: Colors dialog box

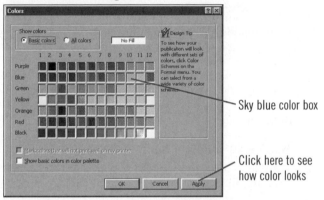

Sky blue color box

Click here to see
how color looks

FIGURE G-7: New color applied to text frame

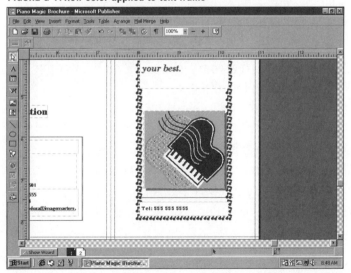

Publisher 2000

Creating a bleed

A bleed is used to make objects look as if they run off the edge of a page, such as section indicators in a book. Because a laser printer uses the edges of the paper to pull the paper in, it is not possible to print all the way to the edge of a page. To make an object appear to run off the edge of a page, you have to trim the page once it has been printed.

Designing WordArt

You have probably seen text in documents and publications that is curved or wavy, to fit a specific shape. You can easily create this effect using WordArt. This program, which is automatically started from within Publisher, gives you a wide variety of text styles and effects from which to choose. Text can be transformed into many shapes, shadows and patterns can be added, and text color can be changed. ▰▰▰▰▰ Marnie wants to add WordArt to the top of the initial panel on page 1, to identify the client's store.

Steps 1234

1. Click the **text frame** at 9" H/1" V, press **[F9]**, right-click the **object**, then click **Delete Object**

   WordArt creates highly stylized text. You can create a WordArt object by using a button on the Objects toolbar.

2. Click the **WordArt Frame Tool button** ▨ on the Objects toolbar, drag the + pointer from 8¼" H/⅝" V to 10" H/1¼" V

   The WordArt window and Enter Your Text Here dialog box open, as shown in Figure G-8. The Publisher toolbar and menu bar are concealed by the WordArt toolbar and WordArt menu bar. The text typed in the Enter Your Text Here text box is displayed in the newly drawn frame.

3. Type **Piano Magic** in the Enter Your Text Here text box, then click **Update Display**

   The display now contains the new text. You can change the font to make the text look more dramatic. Table G-1 shows commonly used WordArt toolbar buttons.

4. Click the **Font list arrow** [Arial ▼] on the WordArt toolbar, scroll the **font list**, then click **Felix Titling**

   The text "Piano Magic" now appears in the Felix Titling font. You can change the shape of the WordArt so the text curves to fill the shape.

5. Click the **Shape list arrow** [— Plain Text ▼] on the WordArt toolbar, then click the **fourth WordArt shape** in the fifth row

   The text takes on the shape. The shape name you selected, Deflate (Bottom), appears in the shape text box. A WordArt shadow adds dimension to the characters within the WordArt object.

6. Click the **Shadow button** ▣ on the WordArt toolbar

   The Shadow dialog box opens, as shown in Figure G-9.

7. Click the **sixth shadow** from the left, then click **OK**

   The dialog box closes and the shadow appears in the text design.

8. Click anywhere on the **scratch area**

   WordArt closes and you are returned to the Publisher window. Compare your page to Figure G-10. Now you zoom out and save your work.

9. Press **[F9]**, then click the **Save button** ▣ on the Standard toolbar

FIGURE G-8: WordArt window

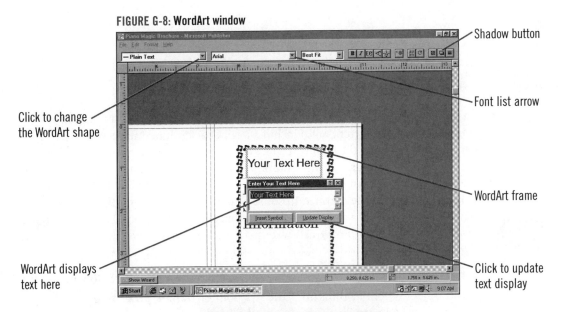

Click to change the WordArt shape

Shadow button

Font list arrow

WordArt frame

WordArt displays text here

Click to update text display

FIGURE G-9: Shadow dialog box in WordArt

Shadow choices

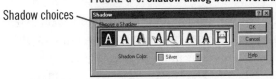

FIGURE G-10: WordArt design in publication

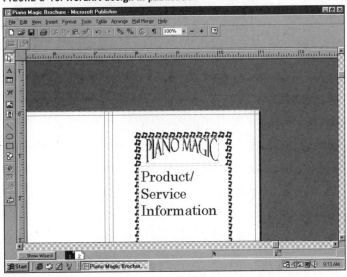

TABLE G-1: Commonly used WordArt toolbar buttons

description	button	description	button
Shape list arrow	— Plain Text ▼	Font list arrow	Arial ▼
Fit list arrow	Best Fit ▼	Bold	**B**
Italic	*I*	Upper/lowercase	Ee
Orientation	◁	Stretch	⬌
Center Align	≣	Character spacing	AV↔
Rotate	↻	Color/Pattern	▨
Shadow	▢	Line width	≡

Creating a Watermark

You have probably seen high-quality paper stock that includes a faint image or text in the background. Some paper currency also includes a faint background image. If you hold a newly issued twenty-dollar bill up to the light you will see a faint image on the right side of the bill. This effect is known as a watermark. A **watermark** is a lightly shaded image that appears behind other objects on a page. It is an effective way of making a statement or identifying a product, mission, or institution in a subtle manner. In some situations, such as a multipage newsletter or poster, you may want to add a watermark to a publication's background page(s). Marnie decides to use the piano image as a watermark in the background.

Steps

1. Press **[Ctrl][M]** to go to the Background, click the **Picture Frame Tool button** 🖼 on the Objects toolbar, then drag the ＋ pointer from **4" H/2" V to 7" H/5" V**
The image you need for the background is on the Project Disk.

2. Right-click the **Picture Frame**, point to **Change Picture**, point to **Picture**, click **From File**, locate your Project Disk, click **piano**, then click **Insert**
The image appears in the frame in the page background.

3. Right-click the **piano image**, point to **Change Picture**, then click **Recolor Picture**
The Recolor Picture dialog box opens, as shown in Figure G-11. You want a light color so that the image will appear faintly on the page.

4. Click the **Color list arrow**, click the **Accent 2 blue color box** in Scheme Colors, then click **OK**
The image changes to the light blue color and appears faintly in the background as a watermark. You can see how the page looks by returning to the foreground view.

5. Press **[Ctrl][M]**
Compare your page to Figure G-12. You can move an object over the watermark later.

6. Click the **Save button** 💾 on the Standard toolbar

FIGURE G-11: **Recolor Picture dialog box**

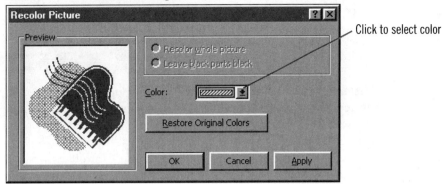

Click to select color

FIGURE G-12: **Clip Art turned into watermark**

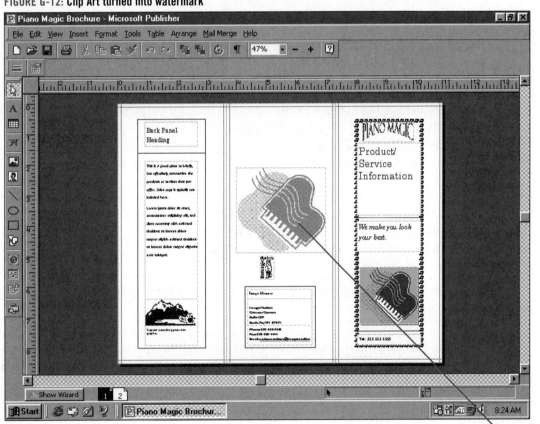

Watermark on
background page

Publisher 2000

Wrapping Text Around a Frame

A story can be made to look interesting by wrapping the text around the frame of an image. This integration of image and text creates a professional look. Depending on the width of an image, a story can appear at the top and bottom or along the sides of an image inserted into a text frame. For added effect, you can make the text flow more closely to the outlines of the graphic image. Two buttons on the Formatting toolbar control text wrap. The Wrap Text to Frame button causes text to wrap around the perimeter of a picture's frame—usually a rectangle. The Wrap Text to Picture button on the Formatting toolbar causes text to wrap around the picture—usually an irregular shape. Marnie has prepared text for the inside fold of the brochure. She would like the text to wrap around the image of a piano.

Steps 1234

1. Right-click the image at **2" H/7" V**, then click **Delete Object**

The placeholder image disappears. You can replace the boilerplate text with your prepared text file.

2. Right-click the **text frame at 2" H/3" V**, point to **Change Text**, click **Text File**, locate the file **Pub G-1** on your Project Disk, then click **OK**

The text file replaces the placeholder text. You can add a clip art image and then shape the text to the object.

3. Click the **Picture Frame Tool button** on the Objects toolbar, drag the + pointer from **1" H/4¾" V** to **1¾" H/5½" V**

The picture frame is inserted midway in the text frame. Use the piano image again.

4. Right-click the **Picture Frame**, point to **Change Picture**, point to **Picture**, click **From File**, click **piano**, click **Insert** then press **[F9]**

The image appears in the frame. Text is broken around the image frame. See Figure G-13. You can turn off the hyphenation feature to keep words from breaking between lines.

Trouble?

Text wrapping may differ slightly depending on the location and size of the image.

5. Click the text frame at **2" H/5" V**, click **Tools** on the menu bar, point to **Language**, click **Hyphenation**, click the **Automatically hyphenate this story check box** to remove the check mark, then click **OK**

The words do not break around the image, and now none of the words in the story are hyphenated.

6. Click the **piano image**, click the **Wrap Text to Picture button** on the Formatting toolbar

The image changes so that the actual shape of the piano rather than the image frame defines the boundaries. The words seem to wrap around this shape, conforming to the contours of the piano. A new formatting toolbar button appears: the Edit Irregular Wrap button.

7. Position the pointer over the **lower-right sizing handle** of the image, drag the pointer to **2" H/5¾" V**

Notice that as the image changes size, the text reforms around it, as shown in Figure G-14.

8. Press **[F9]**, then click the **Save button** on the Standard toolbar

FIGURE G-13: Graphic image inserted in text frame

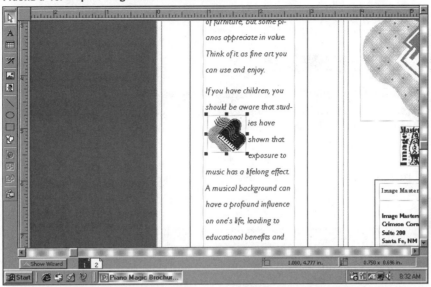

FIGURE G-14: Text wrapped to frame

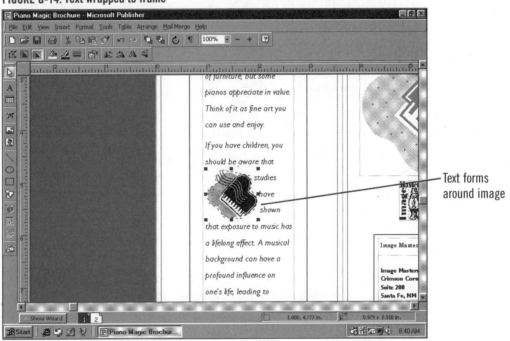

Text forms around image

Editing an irregular shape

Not all figures have perfectly rectangular shapes. Because of these irregular shapes, Publisher lets you display and edit the handles surrounding irregularly shaped frames. Select the image, then click the Edit Irregular Wrap button ▦ on the Formatting toolbar to display each of the handles in such a shape. You can add or delete handles by pressing and holding [Ctrl]. Figure G-15 shows the handles on an irregularly shaped picture. Click and drag any handle so that the text wraps with a more pleasing effect.

FIGURE G-15: Handles surrounding irregularly shaped image

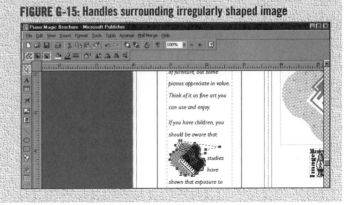

Rotating a Text Frame

WordArt is an effective way of creating special text effects, but you can rotate *any* text frame to create interesting effects using text in a publication. This approach is an effective design technique used to call attention to important text. As you work, you can make use of the scratch area if necessary. Marnie wants to reinforce the message of the brochure by adding a rotated text frame on the last panel of the brochure. She creates the text frame on the scratch area, then rotates it and moves it into position on the page.

Steps 1 2 3 4

1. Right-click the **Image Masters logo object at 5" H/5" V**, then click **Delete Object**
You can create a text frame, add text, and then rotate it on the page.

QuickTip

If necessary, you can use the scratch area to create and design a text frame.

2. Click the **Text Frame Tool button** 🅰 on the Objects toolbar, then drag the ＋ pointer from 3¾" H/5" V to 8¾" H/5½" V
Once the text frame is drawn, you can add your text.

3. Type **Piano Magic: yours to use and enjoy**
The text appears in the frame, but it is too small to be legible.

QuickTip

Headline text should be brief: it is a visual analogy to a sound bite.

4. Press [Ctrl][A], click the **Font list arrow** Times New Roman ▾ on the Formatting toolbar, click **Gill Sans MT**, click the **Font size list arrow** 12 ▾ , then click **24**
Compare your screen to Figure G-16. You can rotate the text frame to any angle.

5. Click the **Custom Rotate button** ↻ on the Standard toolbar; when the Custom Rotate dialog box opens, type **50** in the **Angle text box**, then click **Close**
The text frame is rotated 50 degrees, as seen in Figure G-17. You can drag the text frame into position.

6. Position the pointer on the selected frame; when it changes to ⊕ move the **text frame** so that the top-left edge snaps to the margin guide at 7¼" H/0" V
You want the background of the text frame to be clear, so you can see the watermark. You change the object color of the frame to clear.

7. Click the **Fill Color button** 🖌 on the Formatting toolbar, click **No Fill**, then click the **scratch area**
Compare your work to Figure G-18.

QuickTip

To distinguish your work from others, insert your name in the text box at 4½" H/6" V.

8. Click the **Save button** 💾 on the Standard toolbar, click **File** on the menu bar, click **Print**, click the **Current page option button**, then click **OK**

FIGURE G-16: Text in frame

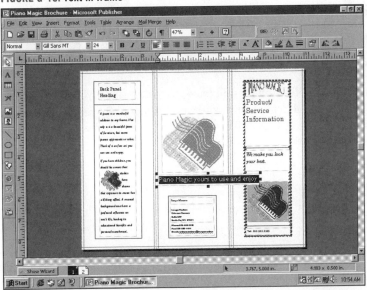

FIGURE G-17: Rotated text frame

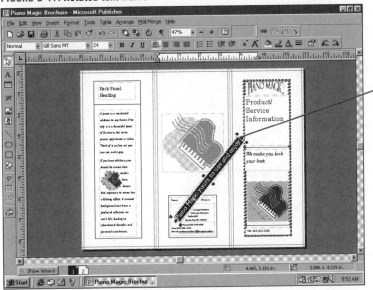

Text frame rotated
50 degrees

FIGURE G-18: Completed rotated text frame

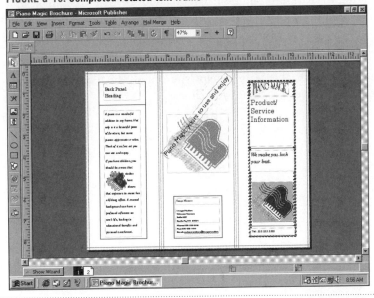

Preparing for Commercial Printing

Publisher 2000

Once your publication is completed, you can print it yourself, or you may want to send the files to a commercial printer for professional results. Marnie knows that once the project is complete, Piano Magic will want the brochure professionally printed. She examines the commercial printing options so she can advise the client and start making arrangements.

Details

Determine the file format
Once the printer is selected, find out the hand-off format. The **hand-off format** is the final format the printer receives. Publisher can create files in the PostScript or Publisher formats.

Explore the PostScript file format
If you choose to send your printer hand-off files in the PostScript format, you will have to install a PostScript printer driver on your computer and save the publication using that printer driver.

You are responsible for updating any necessary graphic images, and including necessary fonts. Ask your commercial printing service if they want you to set any specific print settings. Once the PostScript driver is installed, you can save the publication in the PostScript format. Figure G-19 shows the Save As PostScript File dialog box.

Be aware that due to its large size, you may not be able to save a PostScript file directly to a floppy disk. Try saving to your hard drive, then copying to a floppy disk.

Learn about the Publisher format
If your commercial printing service accepts Publisher format hand-off files, you can take advantage of several important features. The Publisher format verifies linked graphics, embeds TrueType fonts, and packs all the files your printing service might need.

The printing service can use the Publisher format to do **prepress work**. As part of this process, the printer can verify the availability of fonts and linked graphics, make color corrections or separations, and set the final printing options. Figure G-20 shows the Fonts dialog box, and Figure G-21 shows the Graphics Manager dialog box. Each of these dialog boxes gives your printing service important information about elements that make up your publication. If any of these elements is missing, the printer will be able to tell you exactly where the trouble lies.

Take advantage of the Pack and Go Wizard
If you are creating hand-off files using the Publisher format, you can take advantage of the Pack and Go Wizard. This feature helps you put all the files your commercial printing service will need in any type of medium you choose.

FIGURE G-19: Save As PostScript File dialog box

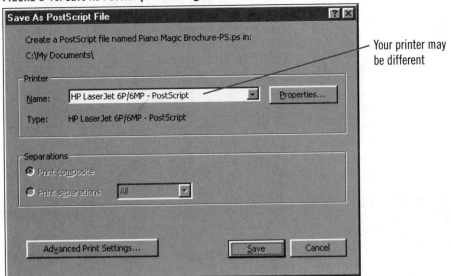

Your printer may be different

FIGURE G-20: Fonts dialog box

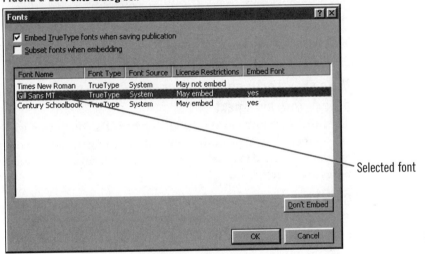

Selected font

FIGURE G-21: Graphics Manager dialog box

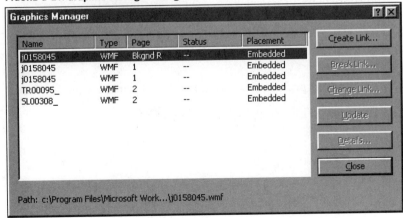

Publisher 2000

Using the Pack and Go Wizard

At some point, you may need to put a publication on disk to take to a commercial printing service, or to use at another computer. Publisher's Pack and Go Wizard lets you package all the fonts and graphic images needed to use your publication elsewhere. ✐━━ Marnie knows that the Piano Magic brochure will be printed by a commercial printing service. Since she has never used the Pack and Go Wizard, she wants to become familiar with it so she can use it easily when necessary.

1. Click File on the menu bar, point to Pack and Go, then click Take to a Commercial Printing Service

The Pack and Go Wizard dialog box opens, as shown in Figure G-22. The first Pack and Go Wizard dialog box explains the advantages of using the Wizard. The items included in the packaged publication file include embedded TrueType fonts and linked graphics. As part of the packing process, the Wizard also prints the publication.

2. Click Next

The second Pack and Go Wizard dialog box lets you determine where you want the packaged files.

3. Make sure the A:\ option button is selected, place a blank formatted floppy disk in drive A, then click Next

The third Pack and Go Wizard dialog box lets you decide what attributes to include. You can embed TrueType fonts, include linked graphics, and create links for embedded graphics, or you can deselect any of these options, if necessary. By default, all three check boxes are selected.

4. Click Next

The fourth Pack and Go Wizard dialog box is shown in Figure G-23. It lets you know the options you've selected, the file-naming scheme it will use, and how to unpack the files.

5. Click Finish

As the Pack and Go Wizard works, you'll see that as the files are being completed, several processes take place. The files are compressed and your publication (Piano Magic Brochure.pub) is saved as Piano Magic BrochurePNG.pub.

Once the publication has been successfully packed, the final Pack and Go Wizard dialog box appears, as seen in Figure G-24.

6. Click OK

As part of the packaging process, the Wizard prints the publication.

7. Click File on the menu bar, then click Exit

FIGURE G-22: First Pack and Go Wizard dialog box

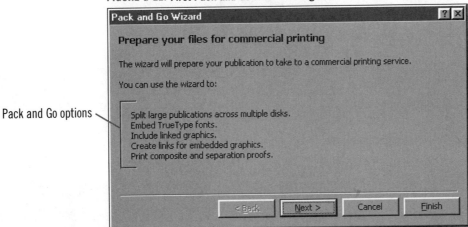

Pack and Go options

FIGURE G-23: Fourth Pack and Go Wizard dialog box

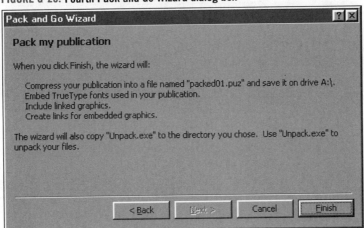

FIGURE G-24: Final Pack and Go Wizard dialog box

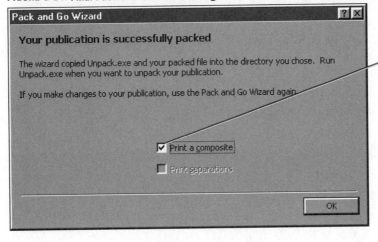

Printing is part
of the packaging
process

Taking files to another computer

Using the Pack and Go Wizard to take a publication to another computer is similar to using it to take a publication to a commercial printing service. To use the Pack and Go Wizard to package files for another computer, click File on the menu bar, point to Pack and Go, and then click Take to Another Computer. Click Next to advance through the dialog boxes, then click Finish at the end.

Practice

► Concepts Review

Label each of the elements of the Publisher window shown in Figure G-25.

FIGURE G-25

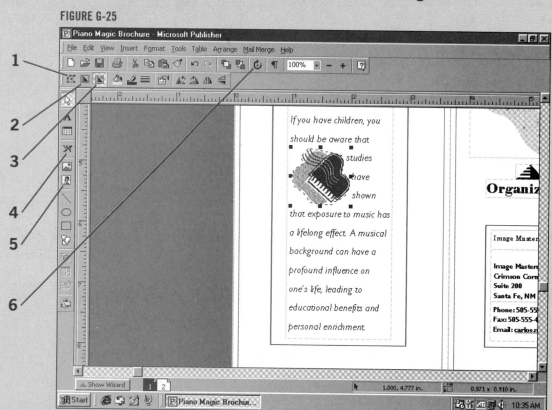

Match each of the buttons with the statement that describes its function.

7.   **a.** Wraps text to frame

8.   **b.** Wraps text to picture

9.   **c.** Creates a WordArt shadow

10.   **d.** Edits irregular shape

11.   **e.** Changes fill color

12.   **f.** Creates WordArt

Select the best answer from the list of choices.

13. **A watermark can be**
    a. Rotated.
    b. Recolored.
    c. Created in the background view.
    d. All of the above

14. **Each of the following is true about WordArt, *except***
    a. The program is started from within Publisher.
    b. WordArt objects can be added only to the foreground view.
    c. WordArt can be resized like any other object.
    d. WordArt can be edited.

15. **Which button is used to create WordArt?**
    a.
    b.
    c.
    d.

16. **Which button is used to rotate an object?**
    a.
    b.
    c.
    d.

17. **Which menu is used to turn off the hyphenation feature?**
    a. File
    b. Format
    c. Tools
    d. Table

18. **Which feature creates curved text?**
    a. TextMaker
    b. WordWinder
    c. Design Checker
    d. WordArt

19. **An object that extends beyond a page's border(s) is called a(n)**
    a. Bleed.
    b. Bleeder.
    c. Edger.
    d. Flow.

20. A lightly shaded image appearing behind other images is called a

    a. Waterbleed.

    b. Watersort.

    c. Watertype.

    d. Watermark.

21. Which button is used to wrap text to a picture?

    a.

    b.

    c.

    d.

▶ Skills Review

Throughout these exercises, use the Zoom feature where necessary.

1. Add BorderArt.

    a. Start Publisher.

    b. Use the Catalog to select the Plain Paper Straight Edge Business Card Wizard. Apply the Monarch color scheme, accept the Landscape orientation, include a logo, print one card in the center of the page, and use the Secondary Business Personal Information set.

    c. Save the file on your Project Disk as Straight Edge Business Card.

    d. Hide the Wizard.

    e. Replace the text at 1" H/¾" V with Straight Edge Engineering, the name of the company whose card you are designing.

    f. Right-click the selected text frame, point to Change Frame, point to Line/Border Style, then click More Styles.

    g. Click the BorderArt tab, then apply the Sawtooth in Gray border. Change the border size to 8 pt, then close the BorderArt dialog box.

    h. Save your work.

2. Create an object shadow.

    a. Make sure the text frame at 1" H/¾" V is selected.

    b. Use the Format menu to apply a shadow to the text frame.

    c. Save your work.

3. Design WordArt.

    a. Delete the object at 2½" H/¾" V. (Click No when asked to change to a design that does not include a logo.)

    b. Click the WordArt Frame Tool button and create a frame from 2½" H/¼" V to 3⅜" H/⅝" V *(snapping to the closest margin guides)*.

    c. Type Cutting Edge Technology.

    d. Change the font to Imprint MT Shadow.

    e. Change the shape to Arch Up (Pour): third row, first on the left.

    f. Click the workspace to return to the publication.

    g. Save your work.

4. **Create a watermark.**
   a. Change to the background view.
   b. Click the Clip Gallery Tool button and create a frame from 1" H/⅜" V to 2½" H/1½" V.
   c. Search on the keyword "enlarges," then insert the image with the filename BD19827_.wmf. Close the Clip Gallery dialog box.
   d. Recolor the picture using the Accent 4 color box.
   e. Change to the foreground view.
   f. Change the fill color of each frame covering the watermark to no fill.
   g. Save the publication.

5. **Wrap text around a frame.**
   a. Click the Clip Gallery Tool button and create a frame from ¼" H/1" V to ¾" H/1 ⅜" V.
   b. Use the Search for clips list arrow to search on the keyword "enlarges," insert the image with the filename BD19827_.wmf, then close the dialog box.
   c. With the image still selected, click the Wrap Text to Picture button.
   d. Save the publication.

6. **Rotate a text frame.**
   a. Draw a new text frame from ½"H/¼" V to 1⅜" H/½" V.
   b. Type "Quality First" in the text frame.
   c. Change the fill color to no fill.
   d. Rotate the text frame 90 degrees.
   e. Move the text frame so that the top-left edge snaps to the closest margin guides at ⅛" H/⅛" V.
   f. Replace the name Carlos Mendoza with your own name and email address. Replace the Image Masters name and address with your own address.
   g. Save your work.

7. **Use the Pack and Go Wizard.**
   a. Open the Pack and Go Wizard to take files to a commercial printing service.
   b. Use an empty, formatted floppy disk, if necessary.
   c. Answer Next to each of the Wizard dialog boxes, then click Finish in the last dialog box.
   d. Hand in the printed publication.
   e. Close the publication.
   f. Exit Publisher.

▶ Independent Challenges

1. As office manager for your company, you've decided to make customized monthly calendars for your company. To complete this independent challenge:

a. Start Publisher and use the Capsules design in the Calendar Wizard.

b. Accept all the defaults.

c. Make the following changes using the Wizard: use the Secondary Business Personal Information set, select the Parrot color scheme, and set the date to the current month, then hide the Wizard.

d. Save the publication as Monthly Calendar on your Project Disk.

e. Add BorderArt around the text frame containing the month and year.

f. Switch to the background view, create a frame with the Clip Gallery Tool button, then add any piece of clip art you choose.

g. Recolor the clip art so it looks like a watermark.

h. Return to the foreground, then modify the fill of any overlapping frames to no fill.

i. Add your name in the e-mail address.

j. Save the publication.

k. Print the publication.

l. Exit Publisher.

2. The Believe It or Not Bookstore has asked you to design a postcard announcing an upcoming event. To complete this independent challenge:

a. Start Publisher and use the Schedule Event design in the Postcard Wizard.

b. Accept all the defaults.

c. Change to Secondary Business Personal Information set, change the color scheme to any scheme you choose, then hide the Wizard.

d. Save the publication as Believe It or Not Postcard on your Project Disk.

e. Change any necessary text to fit the theme of the Believe It or Not Bookstore. Make up a suitable event title.

f. Add BorderArt around the title text frame.

g. Modify the text at 2" H/2" V with your own text.

h. Insert any piece of clip art you choose in the text frame at 2" H/2" V.

i. Wrap the text to the picture.

j. Add your name as the contact person.

k. Use the Pack and Go Wizard to prepare this publication for a commercial printing service. Be sure to prepare a blank formatted disk for drive A.

l. Save the publication.

m. Print the publication.

n. Exit Publisher.

3. Your Publisher skills have convinced you that you can open your own design shop, Design Center. First, you'll need business cards that demonstrate your talent.

To complete this independent challenge:

a. Start Publisher, use any design of your choice in the Business Cards Wizard.

b. Accept all the defaults.

c. Change to the Secondary Business Personal Information set, use any color scheme you choose, then hide the Wizard.

d. Save the publication as Design Center Business Card on your Project Disk.

e. Add BorderArt around a text frame.

f. Switch to the background view, create a frame with the Clip Gallery Tool button, then add any piece of clip art you choose.

g. Recolor the clip art so it looks like a watermark.

h. Return to the foreground, then modify the fill of any overlapping frames to no fill.

i. Create a text frame, type a tag line (of your own invention), then rotate the frame and place it in a strategic location.

j. Add your name, as well as the company name and address to the text frames. (Make up an address, or use your own address.)

k. Save the publication.

l. Print the publication.

m. Exit Publisher.

4. Your employer is interested in having an upcoming publication printed by a commercial printing service. You've told her that Publisher makes it easy to hand off files to such a printer, and you've decided to investigate this capability and create an informative flyer.

To complete this independent challenge:

a. Connect to the Internet and use your browser to go to http://www.microsoft.com. From there, search on Commercial printing with Publisher to find information about Publisher 2000's Commercial Printing Features.

b. Find out the key features and benefits of this Publisher feature and print out any necessary information from the Microsoft Web site.

c. Start Publisher if necessary.

d. Use the Catalog to create a Flyer called Publisher Printing Features.

e. Use bulleted lists to briefly describe the benefits of Publisher's Commercial Printing Features.

f. Add BorderArt to call attention to a frame within the page.

g. Replace any placeholders with your own text.

h. Save the publication.

i. Print the publication.

j. Exit Publisher.

► Visual Workshop

Use the Catalog to create the Accessory Bar Price List Brochure. This is the initial design of a brochure for Tom's Toy Shop. Accept the Wizard defaults, apply the Secondary Business Personal Information set, then change the color scheme to Reef. Save this publication on your Project Disk as Toy Shop Brochure. Use Figure G-26 as a guide. Apply the zig zag pattern BorderArt around the text frame at 9" H/1½" V. Switch to the background view and use the Clip Gallery Tool button to create a frame from ¼" H/2" V to 3¼" H/5" V. Search the Clip Gallery on the keyword "toy trains," then insert the toy train image having the filename HH00526_.wmf. Recolor the background image using the Accent 1 color. (*Hint:* change the fill color of the text frame at 2" H/2" V.) If necessary, replace the store manager's name with your own. Save and print the first page.

FIGURE G-26

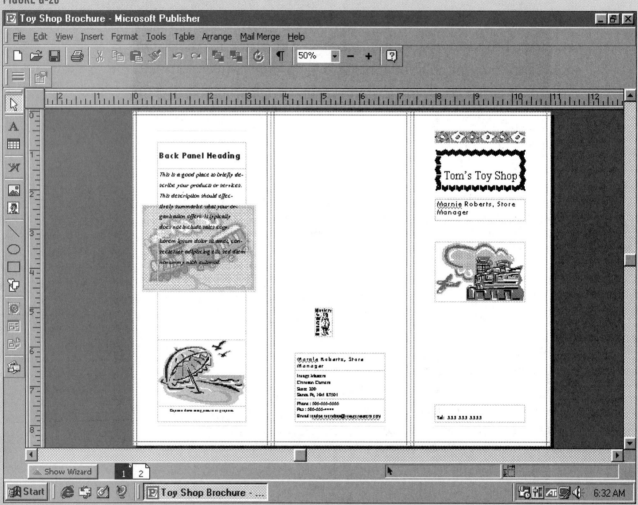

Unit H

Working
on the Web

Objectives

► **Plan a Web site**
► **Use the Web Site Wizard**
► **Add hyperlinks**
► **Modify a background**
► **Add a Design Gallery element**
► **Add an animated GIF**
► **Publish a Web site**
► **Convert a publication into a Web page**

Publisher's enhanced Web capabilities and strong graphics tools make it a great program for creating multipage Web sites. Using Publisher, you can create professional-looking Web sites with attractive backgrounds, useful navigation bars, interesting links, and creative sounds and graphic images—including animated GIFs. Once the Web site is finished, you can publish it so others can access it. ✐ Frank Gonzales is a Web intern for Image Masters. His first project is to experiment with new design ideas for the company's Web site.

Planning a Web Site

Before creating a Web site, it's a good idea to plan the construction of the site, and the elements you want on the page. Although you'll probably make major modifications to your initial design, a solid master plan can help you work more efficiently. ✎ Frank plans the content of Image Masters' Web site.

Details

Create an outline

The first step in preparing a Web site is to prepare an outline. The outline should include a list of all the elements for each page. Information you might want to have on each page includes a title, introductory paragraph, links to other sites, graphic images, sounds, and contact information. For the Image Masters Web site, you want the primary page, or **home page**, to briefly describe Image Masters. You also want a page for the company mission statement, the upcoming Design Clinic, and a listing of satisfied clients.

Decide how many pages are necessary

Before you work on the Web site, you should consider how many pages the site might have. Each page should be linked to the home page, and it should be easy for a reader to jump from page to page. Figure H-1 illustrates relationships that often exist among Web pages.

Add links to other sites

In addition to linking associated pages within your site, you can also provide helpful links to other Web locations of interest to your readers. If you have a page that lists Image Masters clients, you could include links to clients' Web sites.

Add graphics, backgrounds, and design elements

Graphic images enhance any Web page, just as they enhance any publication. A few well-placed images break up blocks of text and make your pages more attractive. You can use any Clip Gallery images in your pages, and Publisher provides over 300 animated GIFs—images with movement—for Web page use. Over 200 backgrounds are provided to make your pages eye-catching, and the Design Gallery contains a variety of elements designed specifically for Web pages. Three additional buttons appear on the Objects toolbar to add Web-related elements.

Save your work

As with any publication, you should save your work often to prevent loss of data. Make sure you have backup copies of any mission-critical work. A good rule of thumb is that you should back up any work you wouldn't want to have to re-create.

Critically examine the page

Because a desktop publishing program always shows you exactly how your page looks, you can monitor your progress as you work. The Image Masters site consists of four pages. Figure H-2 shows the sample Image Masters home page, and Figure H-3 shows the Mission Statement page. Pages 2, 3, and 4 are linked to the home page, and the vertical navigation bar is present on each page, making it easy for a reader to jump to any page in the site. It's a good idea to occasionally step back and imagine that you're seeing your work for the first time. Ask yourself if you find the pages easy to read and navigate.

Test the links

If your pages include links to other Web sites, make sure the links are correct. Periodically check the links to make sure they work as intended.

FIGURE H-1: Possible relationships among Web pages

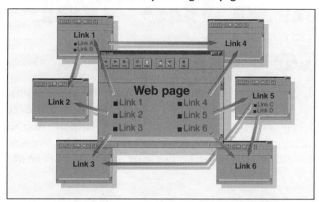

FIGURE H-2: Image Masters home page

Creates a "hot spot"

Creates a form control

Creates an HTML code fragment

Navigation bar

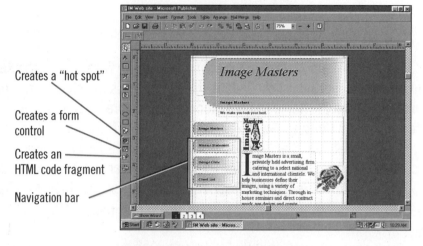

FIGURE H-3: Mission Statement page

Link returns reader to home page

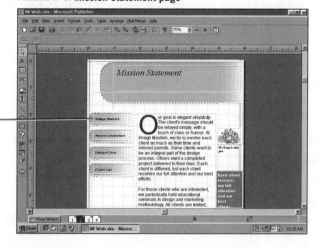

CLUES TO USE

Adding a Hot Spot

A hyperlink—a link to a Web site, document, or e-mail address—can be created for text, an object, or an area within an object. When a hyperlink is confined to an *area within an object* it is called a **hot spot**. You can add multiple hot spots to an object using the Hot Spot Tool button 🔘 on the Objects toolbar. When you click 🔘 the pointer changes to ┼.

Drag ┼ over the area you want as the hot spot. When you release the mouse button, the Hyperlink dialog box opens and you can add any available type hyperlink. In Publisher, a ScreenTip displays the hot spot's hyperlink. In your browser, the hyperlink address displays in the status bar.

Using the Web Site Wizard

The Publisher Catalog contains many types of publications, including those specifically designed as Web sites. Like other Catalog creations, Web sites contain coordinated colors and placeholders for graphic images and text. Additionally, the Web Site Wizard offers navigation bar choices, inclusion of forms, background sounds, and background textures. ✎ Frank will use the Web Site Wizard to get a quick start on his new design ideas.

Steps

1. Start Publisher, click **Web Sites** in the Wizards list, click the **Crisscross Web Site** in the Web Sites list, then click **Start Wizard**
   The Web site is created and appears on the screen. As with other publications, you can use the Wizard to make simple modifications.

2. Click **Finish**, click **Personal Information** in the Web site Wizard, click the **Secondary Business option button**, click **Update**, then, if necessary, change the entries to **Carlos Mendoza** in the Name text box, **Account Executive** in the title text box, **Image Masters, Crimson Corners, Suite 200, Santa Fe, NM, 87501** in the Address text box, **Phone: 505-555-5555, Fax: 505-555-4444, Email** carlos.mendoza@imagemasters.com, in the Phone/fax/e-mail text box, **Image Masters** in the Organization name text box, **We make you look your best.** in the Tag line text box, then click **Update**

3. Click **Hide Wizard** [▼ Hide Wizard], then save the publication as **IM Web Site** on your Project Disk
   You can easily replace text placeholders on this Web page as you would in any publication.

4. Click the **text frame** at 2" H/½" V, press [F9], then type **Image Masters**
   The placeholder is replaced, as shown in Figure H-4. Web sites for a company should include the company logo.

5. Right-click the **picture frame** at 2½" H/2½" V, point to **Change Picture**, point to **Picture**, click **From File**, locate **Im-logo** on your Project Disk, then click **Insert**
   The Image Masters logo replaces the picture placeholder and appears on the page. You can also use images from the Clip Gallery in a Web page.

6. Right-click the **picture frame** at 5" H/5" V, point to **Change Picture**, point to **Picture**, click **Clip Art**, type **paints** in the Search for clips text box, press [Enter], click the image shown in Figure H-5, click the **Insert clip button** 🖼, then click the **Close box** in the Insert Clip Art dialog box
   The placeholder image has been replaced with the image of the paint cans. You can already see how images build a Web page.

7. If necessary, scroll to see the text frame at 4" H/4" V, right-click the **text**, point to **Change Text**, click **Text File**, click **PUB H-1** on your Project Disk, then click **OK**
   The document file replaces the placeholder text. Drop caps work as well as a design element on a Web page as they do in any publication.

8. Click **anywhere in the paragraph**, click **Format** on the menu bar, click **Drop Cap**, click the **choice beneath the current selection**, then click **OK**
   Compare your page to Figure H-6. The Web Site Wizard set up the page nicely, and you were able to replace the placeholders with images and text appropriate for your needs.

9. Click the **Save button** 💾 on the Standard toolbar

FIGURE H-4: Home page placeholder replaced

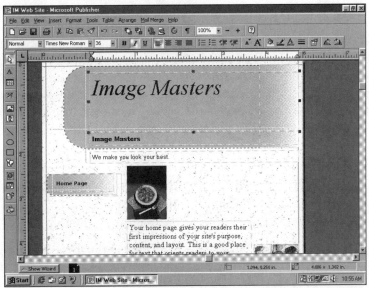

FIGURE H-5: Insert Clip Art dialog box

Use image in
Web page

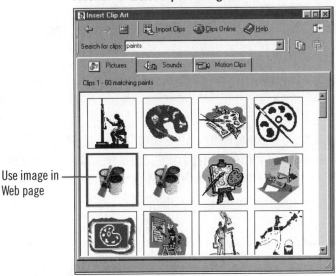

FIGURE H-6: Home page with images and text replaced

Formatted with
a drop cap

Text file in
Web page

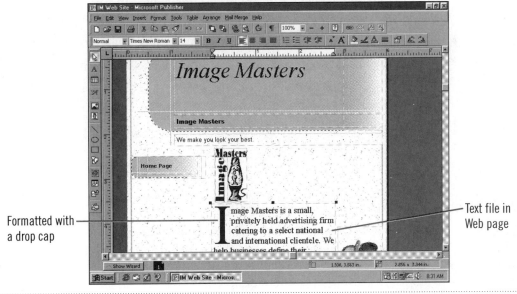

Publisher 2000

Adding Hyperlinks

You use a hyperlink each time you click text in a page and jump to another Web site. Hyperlinks keep the pages within a site just a mouse click away from each other. Links are included in Web pages to make the reader's experience more pleasurable and efficient. You can create links to your own pages, others' Web sites, e-mail addresses, and documents on a specific computer. Pages added to a Web site with a navigation bar are automatically linked. Frank wants to add an additional page to the Web site, and include a link to a client's Web page.

Steps

1. Click ⟦ Show Wizard ⟧ on the Status bar, click **Insert Page** on the Web Site Wizard as shown in Figure H-7, then click **Insert Page**
   The Insert Page dialog box opens. You can choose from a variety of page styles.

QuickTip

Make sure the Add hyperlink to Web navigation bar check box is selected.

2. Click the **Available page types list arrow** in the Insert Page dialog box, scroll the list, click **Related Links**, click **OK**, then click ⟦ Hide Wizard ⟧
   Page 2 is now the current page. The default heading for this page is Directory of Related Links, but this can be changed. There is now a second entry on the navigation bar whose heading is identical to the page title.

3. Click the **text frame** at 2" H/1" V, type **Client Listing**, then press **[Esc]**
   The placeholder text is replaced with the new heading. Notice that the text in the navigation bar is updated to reflect the heading on the page. See Figure H-8. Each page in this Web site has the same navigation bar, and each time a page is added to the site, the navigation bar is updated to include a hyperlink for the new page. The Related Links page style is designed for the inclusion of hyperlinks.

4. Scroll down so you can see the entire **text frame** at 4" H/4" V, click to select the text **Web site name and address hyperlink**, then type **Course Technology**
   The company name, Course Technology, will contain the hyperlink.

5. Select the text **Course Technology**, then click the **Insert Hyperlink button** on the Standard toolbar
   The Hyperlink dialog box opens.

6. Make sure the **A Web site or file on the Internet option button** is selected, click to the **right of http://** in the **Internet address of the Web site or file text box**, type **www.course.com**, as shown in Figure H-9, then click **OK**
   The Course Technology text has changed color and is underlined; It is a hyperlink.

7. Click the **text beneath the Course Technology link**, type **An upscale publisher of high-quality technology textbooks and other electronic training materials.**, then press **[Esc]**
   Compare your page to Figure H-10.

8. Click the **Save button** on the Standard toolbar

Adding a hyperlink to an e-mail address

By adding a hyperlink to an e-mail address, you can make it easy for your readers to keep in touch. Once the Hyperlink dialog box is open, click the Internet e-mail address option button, enter a valid address in the Internet e-mail address text box, then click OK.

FIGURE H-7: Web Site Wizard

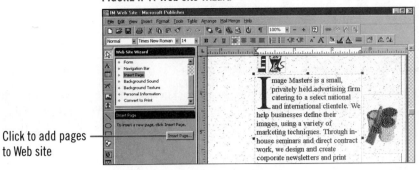

Click to add pages
to Web site

FIGURE H-8: New page added to Web site

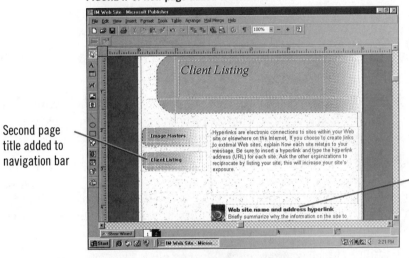

Second page
title added to
navigation bar

Hyperlink can be
inserted here

FIGURE H-9: Hyperlink dialog box

Hyperlink options

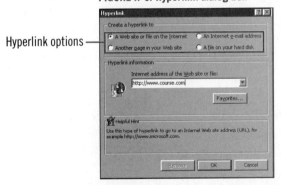

FIGURE H-10: New page with hyperlink added

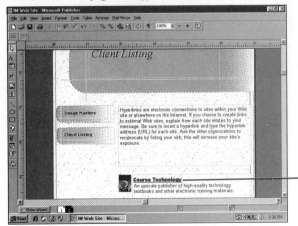

Blue underlined text
indicates a hyperlink

Publisher 2000

Modifying a Background

Backgrounds enhance a Web page. The textured background of the pages in the Web site can be modified to have a different texture or none at all. You can modify the background texture using the Web backgrounds provided in Publisher. Frank wants to modify the background texture.

1. Click the **page 1 icon** on the status bar, then click [△ Show Wizard] on the status bar
   The Web Site Wizard opens.

2. Click **Background Texture** in the Web Site Wizard, then click **Select Texture**
   The Color and Background Scheme dialog box opens, as shown in Figure H-12. You can use this dialog box to change the color scheme in the Web site, as well as the background texture.

> **Trouble?**
> Your default View button may be List, Details, Properties, or Preview.

3. Click **Browse**, click the **Views button list arrow**, then click the **Preview button** ▣
   The Web Backgrounds dialog box opens, as shown in Figure H-13. The background files are named in such a way that the file names give you no insight to a background's appearance, but the Preview pane helps you pick your background. You want to select a deeper shade for the background—one that will make the text stand out.

4. Click **WB00516I**, click **Open**, click **OK**, then click [▼ Hide Wizard]
   The page has a beige textured background, as shown in Figure H-14.

CLUES TO USE

Creating a custom color scheme

You can create your own custom color schemes just like those included in the Publisher color scheme list. Custom color schemes include main, accent, and hyperlink colors as well as background textures. You create a custom color scheme by making selections using the Web Site Wizard. Click the Select Texture button, then click the Custom tab in the Color and Background Scheme dialog box as shown in Figure H-11. Click the list arrows for any of the Scheme colors in the New column, then click a color from the palette. When all your selections are made, you can name the scheme by clicking the Save Scheme button, typing a name for the scheme, then clicking OK. Click OK to close the Color and Background Scheme dialog box as shown in Figure H-11. Now the color scheme is available for future use.

FIGURE H-11: Custom tab in the Color and Background Scheme dialog box

Select new color choices using list arrows

FIGURE H-12: Color and Background Scheme dialog box

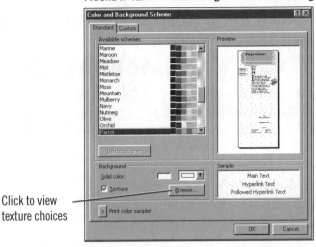

Click to view
texture choices

FIGURE H-13: Web Backgrounds dialog box

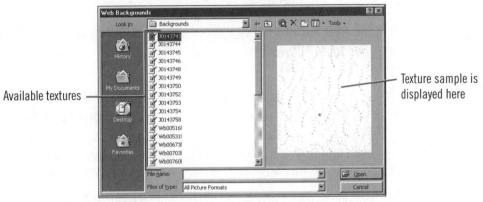

Available textures

Texture sample is
displayed here

FIGURE H-14: Web page background texture modified

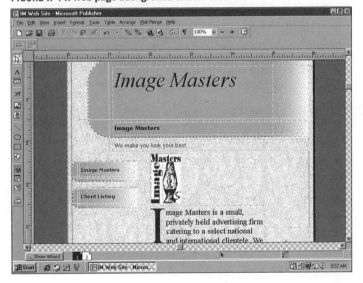

Publisher 2000

Adding a Design Gallery Element

There is a wide variety of elements such as mastheads, navigation bars, buttons, reply forms, sidebars, and pull quotes designed especially for Web pages. These additional elements are found in the Design Gallery. Although you can use any Publisher element in a Web page, these images are specifically designed for Web use. ✐━━ Frank wants to include an e-mail hyperlink that makes it easy for readers to contact the Webmaster.

Steps 1 2 3 4

1. Scroll down the screen until **1" H/7" V** is visible, then click the **Design Gallery Object button** 🖼 on the Objects toolbar

   The Design Gallery dialog box opens, as shown in Figure H-15. Notice that there are six categories specifically for Web pages.

2. Click the **Web Buttons category**, click **Email Half Capsule** from the Web buttons list, then click **Insert Object**

   The Web button object is placed on the page.

Trouble?
If you get a message that the object is too close to another object on the page, move the object to the correct location.

3. Position the pointer over the **Web button object**, when the pointer changes to ⬆, press the left mouse button, then drag the **Web button object** so the top-left edge is at ½" H/6½" V

   The e-mail button is in its new location. You can add a hyperlink to this image so users can click the image to send an e-mail message to the address you specify.

4. Right-click the **Web button object**, then click **Hyperlink**

   The Hyperlink dialog box opens.

5. Click the **An Internet e-mail address option button**, press [Tab], type **webmaster@ imagemasters.com**, as shown in Figure H-16, then click **OK**

   Although it looks as if nothing has happened, the hyperlink information is entered for this object.

6. Click the **scratch area**

   Compare your page to Figure H-17.

7. Click the **Save button** 💾 on the Standard toolbar

FIGURE H-15: Design Gallery dialog box with Web page categories

Web-specific elements

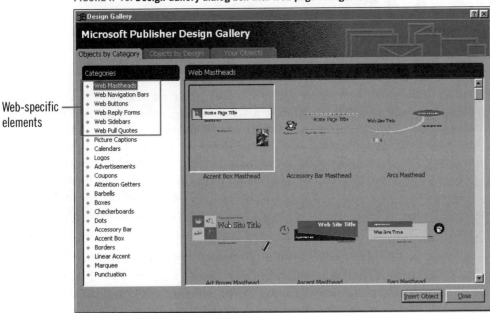

FIGURE H-16: Hyperlink dialog box

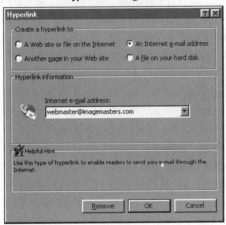

FIGURE H-17: Hyperlinked Web button

Clicking this button in browser will open an e-mail window

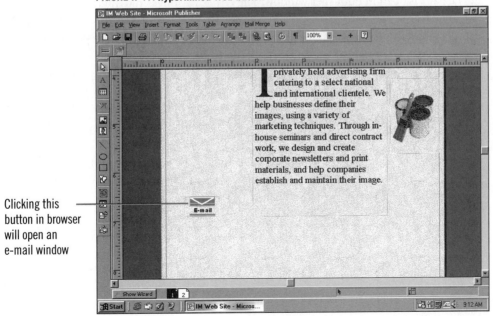

Publisher 2000

Adding an Animated GIF

A moving object on a Web page is one sure way to attract attention. You can create moving images on your page using an animated GIF. The **GIF** format—which stands for **Graphics Interchange Format**—is commonly used on the Web because of its small file size. This format is displayed *natively* by most browsers (meaning that it is displayed without the use of additional programs). The animation will not be visible in Publisher; you have to view the animated GIF in a browser to see the movement. Its small size means it is quickly downloaded from the Web. Frank knows an animated GIF will generate additional interest in the page. He has downloaded from Microsoft's Clip Gallery Live Web site the animated GIF that he wants to use.

1. Click the **Picture Frame Tool button** 🖼 on the Objects toolbar, then drag the + pointer from ½" H/5" V to 1¼" H/5¾" V
   The image file will go in the picture frame. Animated GIFs downloaded from Microsoft's Clip Gallery Live Web site have numerically coded filenames.

2. Right-click the **picture frame**, point to **Change Picture**, point to **Picture**, click **From File**, locate the **J0223749(t)** file on your Project Disk, then click **Insert**
   Compare your page to Figure H-18. The image looks static, no different from any other image on the page, until you see the page in a browser capable of viewing an animated GIF.

QuickTip

Animated GIFs can be added to the Clip Gallery.

3. Click the **Web Page Preview button** 🔍 on the Standard toolbar
   The Web page is prepared for viewing in the default Web browser. If Internet Explorer is installed on your system, the page opens in IE.

Trouble?

If the animated GIF is not moving, your browser may not have this capability.

4. Scroll down the browser screen until the animated GIF is visible
   Compare your screen to Figure H-19. You should see a man running while the hands of the clock spin.

QuickTip

To distinguish your work from that of others, draw a one-inch square text box below the e-mail button, then type "prepared by *your name*."

5. Click **File** on the browser menu bar, then click **Close**
   The Page is open in Publisher window. The GIF is no longer moving.

6. Click the **Save button** 💾 on the Standard toolbar, click **File** on the menu bar, click **Print**, click the **Current page option button**, then click **OK**

FIGURE H-18: Animated GIF on page

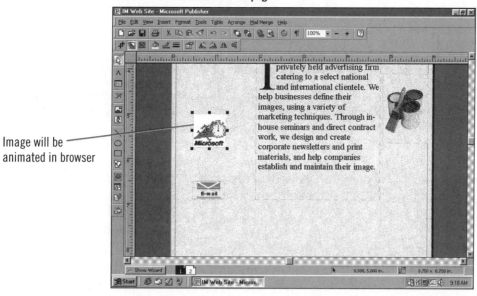

Image will be animated in browser

FIGURE H-19: Animated GIF in browser

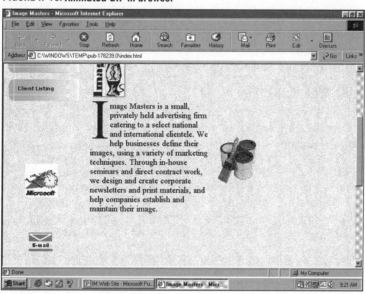

Adding sound clips to a Web page

You can add sounds to your Web pages, and readers of your page who have sound-capable computers will be able to hear them when the page opens. You can install most commonly used sound formats. To install a background sound, click the Show Wizard button [Show Wizard], click Background Sound, then click Browse. The Web Properties dialog box opens. Click the Background sound File name list arrow, click a sound file on your computer, as shown in Figure H-20, then click OK. The sound file will play as soon as the page is opened.

FIGURE H-20: Web Properties dialog box

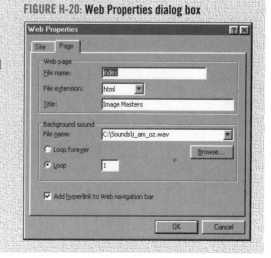

Publisher 2000

Publisher 2000

Publishing a Web Site

Once your Web site is finished, it needs to be published on the Web so others can see it. Publisher offers several ways you can do this. Before you can publish a Web site to the Web, you must create a Web folder for the site. A **Web folder** is a shortcut to a location on a Web server where your pages will reside. Before beginning the publishing process, you must get a URL (Uniform Resource Locator) from your ISP (Internet Service Provider). ▄▄▄▄ Once the Image Masters Web site is complete, it will need to be published to the Web. Frank researches the steps required to do this, so he will be familiar with the procedure.

Details

Create Web folder

The first step in creating a Web folder is to contact your Internet provider and get an address for your files. Once this is complete, double-click My Computer on the Windows desktop, double-click Web Folders, double-click Add Web Folder, then follow the instructions in the Add Web Folder Wizard to complete this process.

Save the publication as a Web page

To save the publication as a Web page, you need to use the Save As Web Page dialog box shown in Figure H-21, which is available from the File menu. Open Web Folders then locate the folder in which you want your files published.

Use the Web Publishing Wizard

You can use Microsoft's Web Publishing Wizard to facilitate the process. This program is available through a custom installation of Internet Explorer 5. If the Web Publishing Wizard does not appear on your Programs menu, you may need to reinstall Internet Explorer.

The first Web Publishing Wizard dialog box is shown in Figure H-22. You will have to know the location of the file or folder you want to publish, and you must type a name for the Web site in the Descriptive name text box. You will be asked to type the URL you received from your ISP in the URL or Internet address text box, and verify the local directory, as shown in Figure H-23. After an Internet connection is established, you must select a connection method and verify the server name, and then your files will be published to the server name you specified.

FIGURE H-21: Save As Web Page dialog box

Location for Web site files

FIGURE H-22: First Web Publishing Wizard dialog box

FIGURE H-23: Fourth Web Publishing Wizard dialog box

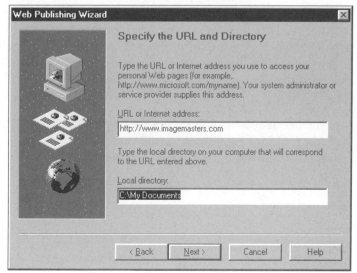

Publisher 2000

Publisher 2000

Converting a Publication into a Web Page

A Publisher-designed newsletter or brochure (one created using the Catalog) can be converted into a Web page with the same wizard used in the modification process. When a publication is converted to a Web site, you can use the Web Site Wizard to automatically create a design with hyperlinks. If you prefer, you can design your own layout and create your own hyperlinks. Any newsletter or brochure Frank develops may ultimately be converted to a Web page. Frank knows this and wants to review the conversion process. He uses the Catalog to quickly create a brochure he can use for practice.

Steps

1. Click **File** on the menu bar, click **New**, click **Brochures** in the Wizards list, click **Informational**, click **Blends Informational Brochure**, then click **Start Wizard**
   The brochure is created and appears on the screen.

2. Click **Finish**, click **Personal Information** in the Brochure Wizard, then click the **Secondary Business** option button

3. Click **Color Scheme** in the Brochure Wizard, click **Parrot** in the Color Scheme list, click the **Save button** 🖫, type **Brochure Conversion** in the File name text box, then click **Save**
   The publication is saved on your Project Disk. The last choice in the upper frame of the Brochure Wizard is Convert to Web. You can use this choice to turn your brochure into a Web site.

4. Click the text frame at **9" H/3" V**, type **Image Masters Brochure**, press [Esc], then click 🖫 on the Standard toolbar
   Your screen should look like Figure H-24.

QuickTip

You can convert publications other than Publisher-designed brochures and newsletters to Web pages by copying and pasting content to Web pages.

5. Click **Convert to Web** in the Brochure Wizard, then click **Create**
   The Convert To Web Site dialog box is displayed, as shown in Figure H-25.

6. Make sure the **Use the Web Site Wizard to automatically create a Web design with hyperlinks option button** is selected, then click **OK**
   Compare your screen to Figure H-26. Your brochure has been converted into a new, unnamed Web site. Some elements had to be removed because they didn't fit the current design. Design elements removed during a conversion process are always saved and available for viewing using the Extra Content button. Removed objects are added to the Extra Content tab in the Design Gallery.

7. Save the publication as **Converted Web Site** on your Project Disk, then click **Exit**
   While the converted publication has the same file format as the brochure before conversion, its pages are organized using a Web page format.

FIGURE H-24: Brochure before conversion

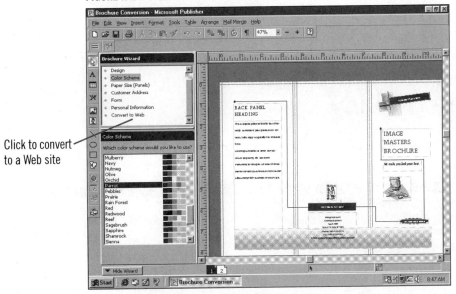

Click to convert to a Web site

FIGURE H-25: Convert To Web Site dialog box

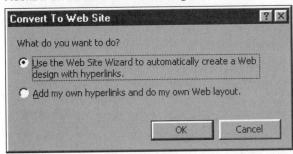

FIGURE H-26: Publication converted to Web site

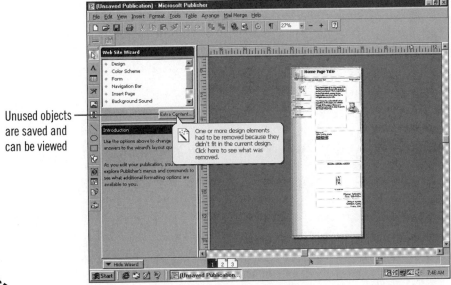

Unused objects are saved and can be viewed

CLUES TO USE

Converting a Web site to a print publication

You can also convert a Publisher-designed Web site (one created using the Catalog) into a brochure or newsletter. Once the Web site you want to convert is open, click the Show Wizard button on the Status bar. Click the Convert to Print option, then click the type of print publication you want.

Practice

► Concepts Review

Label each of the elements of the Publisher window shown in Figure H-27.

FIGURE H-27

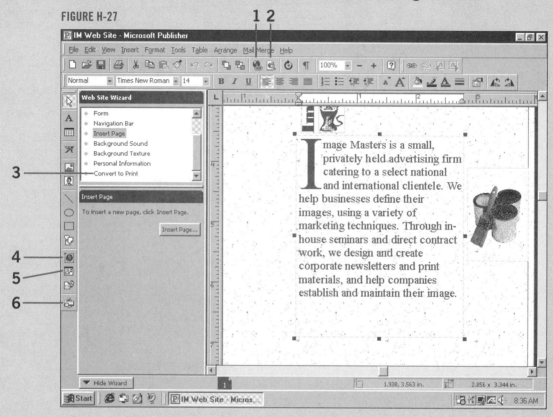

Match each of the buttons or terms with the statement that describes its function.

7.   a. Views page in browser
8.   b. Creates a hyperlink
9.   c. Creates Web forms
10.   d. Contains Web design elements
11.   e. Creates a frame for an animated GIF
12.   f. Creates a hot spot

Select the best answer from the list of choices.

13. Each of the following is true about a navigation bar, *except*
   a. It is created by the Web Site Wizard.
   b. It can contain an animated GIF.
   c. It can be horizontal or vertical in design.
   d. It is automatically updated when a page is added.

14. Add sound clips to a Web page using the
   a. Programs menu.
   b. Objects toolbar.
   c. Format menu.
   d. Web Site Wizard.

15. Which button is used to add a hyperlink?
   a.
   b.
   c.
   d.

16. Which of the following can you create hyperlinks to on a Web page?
   a. Other Web sites
   b. E-mail addresses
   c. Web pages in your own Web site
   d. All of the above

17. Modify a Web page's background texture using the
   a. Web Site Wizard.
   b. Edit menu.
   c. Format menu.
   d. All of the above.

18. Which statement about hyperlinks is true?
   a. You can add a hyperlink to any object.
   b. The only object to which you can add a hyperlink is an animated GIF.
   c. You cannot add a hyperlink to a text frame.
   d. A hyperlink cannot be used with e-mail.

19. GIF stands for
   a. Great Image Format.
   b. Graphics Interchange Format.
   c. Good Image Format.
   d. None of the above.

20. Which statement is true about animated GIFs?
   a. They only display movement in a browser.
   b. They display movement in Publisher and a browser.
   c. They cannot be added to the Clip Gallery.
   d. They are available for a fee from Microsoft's Clip Gallery Live.

21. Which button is used to add Web design elements?
   a.
   b.
   c.
   d.

Skills Review

Throughout these exercises, use the Zoom feature, and hide and show the Wizard, when necessary. If you are using a floppy disk to save your completed publications, you need to copy the following files to another floppy disk in order to complete the end-of-unit material for this unit: J0178166(t).gif, J0178166.cil, Canyon.tif, DSNGRR.tif.

1. **Use the Web Site Wizard.**
   a. Start Publisher.
   b. Use the Catalog to create a Web Site for Ladders By Mail. Select the Bubbles Web Site Wizard, accept all the Wizard defaults, use the Secondary Business Personal Information set, and apply the Shamrock color scheme.
   c. Save the file on your Project Disk as Ladders By Mail Web Site.
   d. Replace the title home page text at 2" H/1" V with Ladders By Mail.
   e. Replace the text in the frame at 5" H/1½" V with "*Your Name*, Owner."
   f. Save your work.

2. **Add hyperlinks.**
   a. Use the Web Site Wizard to insert a Related Links page after the home page. (Make sure the hyperlink is added to the navigation bar.)
   b. Change the title of page 2 (at 2" H/1" V) to Happy Customers.
   c. Click the text frame at 4" H/4" V, make sure the Web site name and address hyperlink text are selected, then type Microsoft Corporation.
   d. Select the Microsoft Corporation text, then click the Insert Hyperlink button on the Standard toolbar.
   e. Make sure the Web site or file on the Internet option button is selected, enter the Internet address http://www.microsoft.com, then click OK.
   f. Save your work.

3. **Modify a background.**
   a. Click Background Texture in the Web Site Wizard, then click Select Texture.
   b. Click Browse in the Background texture area of the Standard tab.
   c. Click J0143750, click Open, then click OK.
   d. Save your work.

4. **Add a Design Gallery element.**
   a. Click the page 1 icon.
   b. Click the Design Gallery Object button, then click the Web Buttons category.
   c. Click the Email Token Web Button, then click Insert Object.
   d. Drag the object so the upper-left edge is at ¼" H/5" V.
   e. Click the Insert Hyperlink button on the Standard toolbar, make sure the An Internet e-mail address option button is selected, type your e-mail address in the Internet e-mail address text box, then click OK.
   f. Save the publication.

5. Add an animated GIF.

   a. Delete the graphic image object at 5" H/3" V.

   b. Click the Picture Frame Tool button on the Objects toolbar, then create a frame from 5" H/3" V to 5¾" H/3¾" V.

   c. Right-click the frame, point to Change Picture, point to Picture, then click From File.

   d. Locate the file J0178166(t) on your Project Disk, then click Insert.

   e. Save the publication, then click the scratch area.

   f. Click the Web Page Preview button on the Standard toolbar. Notice the animated GIF image. The animation is of the man climbing the ladder.

   g. Print the browser page, then close the browser window.

6. Convert a publication into a Web page.

   a. Use the Catalog to create a Brochure for Ladders By Mail. Select the Bubbles Informational Brochure Wizard, accept all the Wizard defaults, use the Secondary Business Personal Information set, and apply the Shamrock color scheme.

   b. Save the file on your Project Disk as Ladders By Mail Brochure.

   c. Click Convert to Web.

   d. Click Create. (Make sure the Web Site Wizard automatically creates a design with hyperlinks.)

   e. Save the new publication as Ladder Conversion.

   f. Print page 1 of the Web site.

   g. Close the publication.

   h. Exit Publisher.

► Independent Challenges

1. As the proud owner of a very successful comic book store in Binghamton, NY, you have decided to expand your store Comix Alive, which specializes in rare comic books, by designing a Web site. This way, you will be able to retain as customers all the university students who leave town after graduating.

   To complete this independent challenge:

   a. Start Publisher, use the Blocks Web Site design in the Web Site Wizard.

   b. Accept all the defaults.

   c. Make the following changes using the Wizard: Secondary Business Personal Information set, Wildflower color scheme. Then hide the wizard.

   d. Save the publication as Comix Alive Web Site on your Project Disk.

   e. Change the title of the home page to Comix Alive.

   f. Insert a Related Links page after the Home Page.

   g. Select the first Web site name and address hyperlink text listed on page 2.

   h. Create a hyperlink to any other comic book site. (Make up a site if you are unfamiliar with related sites.)

   i. Use the Design Gallery Object button to add a Web button. Add a hyperlink to the button, containing your name.

   j. If necessary, add a text frame containing your name on page 1.

   k. Save the publication.

   l. Print the publication.

   m. Exit Publisher.

2. Your family has asked you to create a newsletter that can be distributed to all its members, and you know that a request for a Web site won't be far behind. Thinking ahead, you want to prepare a simple mock-up of a family newsletter, convert it to a Web site, then suggest it to the family at its next gathering.

To complete this independent challenge:

a. Start Publisher, use any design in the Newsletter Wizard.

b. Accept all the defaults.

c. Change to Secondary Business Personal Information set, then change the colors to your choice of schemes.

d. Save the publication as Family Newsletter on your Project Disk.

e. Make modifications you feel are necessary to give family members a feel for the newsletter, but make sure the newsletter masthead contains your last name. (For example, the masthead might be "Gonzales Gazette.")

f. If you wish, you can replace any images with clip art or artwork at your disposal.

g. Save your work and print the first page of the newsletter.

h. Use the Newsletter Wizard to convert the publication to a Web site, having the Web Site Wizard automatically create a design with hyperlinks.

i. Save the converted file as Family Web Site on your Project Disk.

j. Use the Design Gallery Object button to add a Web button on the home page.

k. Create a hyperlink to the Web button that allows a user to send e-mail to you.

l. Save the Web site.

m.Print the Web site's home page.

n. Exit Publisher.

3. You have been hired to create a Web site for Jack's Joke Shop. This company has been in business for years, and would like to have a Web presence.

To complete this independent challenge:

a. Start Publisher, use any design of your choice in the Web Sites Wizard.

b. Accept all the defaults.

c. Change to the Secondary Business Personal Information set and use any color scheme you choose.

d. Save the publication as Joke Shop Web Site on your Project Disk.

e. Use the Web Site Wizard to change the background texture to any texture you choose.

f. Insert an event page after the home page.

g. Enter your name as a speaker on the event page, then create a hyperlink to your e-mail address.

h. Change the title of the event page, then verify that the hyperlink to that page changes.

i. Make any changes to the text that you feel are necessary.

j. Save the publication.

k. Print page 2 of the publication.

l. Exit Publisher.

4. You have seen how dynamic Web sites look when they contain animated GIFs, and you have convinced your boss that they would look great in the company's Web site.
To complete this independent challenge:

a. Log on to the Internet and use your browser to go to http://www.microsoft.com. From there, locate the Microsoft Clip Gallery Live Web site.

b. Locate and download a motion clip you find appealing.

c. Start Publisher if necessary.

d. Use the Catalog to create any Web site design you choose, using the Secondary Business Personal Information set, and any color scheme.

e. Save the publication as Animated Web Site on your Project Disk.

f. Modify the home page title to include your name.

g. Change the background texture of the Web site.

h. Create a picture frame somewhere on the home page.

i. Insert the animated GIF in the picture frame.

j. Save the publication.

k. View the Web site using your browser.

l. Print the Web site in your browser.

m. Exit the browser and Publisher.

▶ ## Visual Workshop

Use the Catalog to create the Southwest Web Site. Save this publication on your Project Disk as Traveler Web Site. Accept the Wizard defaults, apply the Secondary Business Personal Information set, then change the color scheme to Bluebird. Using Figure H-28 as a guide, add two additional story pages (Colorado Adventures and New Mexico Adventures). Insert the images Canyon and DSNGRR (both included on your Project Disk). Replace any text, using Figure H-28 as a guide. If necessary, include your name in a text box on page 1, then print page 1.

FIGURE H-28

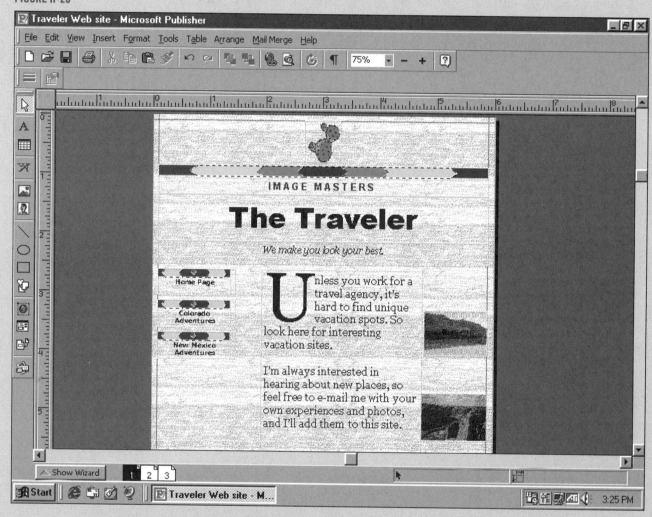

Project Files List

Note: File sizes for Independent Challenges are approximate. Actual file sizes may be either larger or smaller.

Unit	File names	File size	Saved as	File size	Used in	Notes
Unit A	PUB A-1	61 KB	Grand Opening flyer	62 KB	Lesson 4-8	
	PUB A-2	27 KB	Sample Business Card	29 KB		
			Suggestion 1,	19 KB	Independent Challenge 2	
			Suggestion 2,	17 KB		
			Suggestion 3,	19 KB		
			Explanation	21 KB		
	PUB A-3	37 KB	IM-Award	37 KB	Independent Challenge 3	
	PUB A-4	50 KB	Image Masters Gift Card	50 KB	Visual Workshop	
Total		175 KB		254 KB		
Unit B			IM Newsletter	186 KB	Lessons	Create with Catalog
	PUB B-1	20 KB			Lessons	Word file inserted into publication
	IM-Logo.TIF	4 KB			Lessons	TIF file inserted into publication
	PUB B-2	19 KB			Lessons	Word file inserted into publication
			Mock-up Newsletter	144 KB	Skills Review	Create with Catalog
	PUB B-3	20 KB			Skills Review	Word file inserted into publication
	PUB B-4	19 KB			Skills Review	Word file inserted into publication
			Fun Walk Flyer	38 KB	Independent Challenge 1	Create with Catalog
			Take-Out Menu	89 KB	Independent Challenge 2	Create with Catalog
			For Rent Sign	22 KB	Independent Challenge 3	Create with Catalog
			Publisher Class Web Page	248 KB	Independent Challenge 4	Create with Catalog
			IM Postcard	44 KB	Visual Workshop	Create with Catalog
Total		82 KB		771 KB		

Unit	File names	File size	Saved as	File size	Used in	Notes
Unit C			Design Clinic Flyer	42 KB	Lessons	Create with Catalog
	PUB C-1	19 KB			Lessons	Word file inserted into publication
			Company Picnic Flyer	42 KB	Skills Review	Create with Catalog
	PUB C-2	19 KB			Skills Review	Word file inserted into publication
			My Promotion Invitation	33 KB	Independent Challenge 1	Create with Catalog
			Leadership Seminar Certificate	30 KB	Independent Challenge 2	Create with Catalog
			Music Program	150 KB	Independent Challenge 3	Create with Catalog
			KLIC Web Page	49 KB	Independent Challenge 4 (WWW)	Create with Catalog
			Estate Sale Flyer	32 KB	Visual Workshop	Create with Catalog
Total		38 KB		378 KB		
Unit D			Fund-raiser Flyer	189 KB	Lessons	Create with Catalog
			Family Picnic Postcard	170 KB	Skills Review	Create with Catalog
			New IM Card Design	33 KB	Independent Challenge 1	Create with Catalog
			Gift Certificate	35 KB	Independent Challenge 2	Create with Catalog
			Current Calendar	33 KB	Independent Challenge 3	Create with Catalog
			Luggable Luggage	252 KB	Independent Challenge 4 (WWW)	Create with Catalog
			Party Invitation	62 KB	Visual Workshop	Create with Catalog
Total				774 KB		
Unit E			Route 66 Traveler	458 KB	Lessons	Create with Catalog
	PUB E-1	19 KB			Lessons	Word file inserted into publication
	Sunset.tif	41 KB			Lessons	TIF file
	PUB E-2	20 KB			Lessons	Word file inserted into publication
			Santa Fe Newsletter	126 KB	Skills Review	Create with Catalog
	PUB E-3	21 KB			Skills Review	Word file inserted into publication
			Finance Wizardry Brochure	79 KB	Independent Challenge 1	

Unit	File names	File size	Saved as	File size	Used in	Notes
			Community Promotion Newsletter	173 KB	Independent Challenge 2	
			Special Event	20 KB		Word file inserted into publication
			Animal Shelter Flyer	116 KB	Independent Challenge 3	
			Maine Leaves Brochure	87 KB	Independent Challenge 4 (WWW)	
			Maine Attractions	20 KB		Word file inserted into publication
	PUB E-4	19 KB	SW Brochure	566 KB	Visual Workshop	
	PUB E-5	21 KB				
	Rabbit.tif	22 KB				
	Balloons.tif	55 KB				
	Canyon.tif	58 KB				
	Spider.tif	40 KB				
Total		316 KB		1645 KB		
Unit F			Rug Catalog	206 KB	Lessons	Create with Catalog
	Wruins-1.tif	56 KB			Lessons	TIF file inserted into publication
	PUB F-1	20 KB			Lessons	Word file inserted into publication
	Wruins-2.tif	67 KB		171 KB	Lessons	TIF file inserted into publication
	PUB F-2	19 KB				Word file inserted into publication
			Video Store Catalog	76 KB	Skills Review	Create with Catalog
			Video Label	23 KB	Skills Review	Create with Catalog
			Play Program	63 KB	Independent Challenge 1	Create with Catalog
			School Newsletter	380 KB	Independent Challenge 2	Create with Catalog
			Personal Shipping Label	25 KB	Independent Challenge 3	Create with Catalog
			Publisher Newsletter	200 KB	Independent Challenge 4	Create with Catalog
			Rug Collection Binder	316 KB	Visual Workshop	TIF file inserted into publication
	Yeirug.tif	116 KB				TIF file inserted into publication
Total		278 KB		1460 KB		

Unit	File names	File size	Saved as	File size	Used in	Notes
Unit G			Piano Magic Brochure	225 KB	Lessons	Create with Catalog
	PUB G-1	19 KB			Lessons	
			Straight Edge Business Card	137 KB	Skills Review	Create with Catalog
			Monthly Calendar	53 KB	Independent Challenge 1	Create with Catalog
			Believe It or Not Postcard	32 KB	Independent Challenge 2	Create with Catalog
			Design Center Business Card	21 KB	Independent Challenge 3	Create with Catalog
			Publisher Printing Features	150 KB	Independent Challenge 4	Create with Catalog
			Toy Shop Brochure	106 KB	Visual Workshop	Create with Catalog
Total		19 KB		574 KB		
Unit H			IM Web Site	884 KB	Lessons	Create with Catalog
	PUB H-1	19 KB			Lessons	Word file inserted into publication
	Im-logo.tif	4 KB			Lessons	TIF file inserted into publication
	J0223749(t).gif	9 KB			Lessons	Animated GIF inserted into publication
			Brochure Conversion	63 KB	Lessons	Create with Catalog
			Converted Web Site	117 KB	Lessons	Create with Catalog
			Ladders By Mail Web Site	100 KB	Skills Review	Create with Catalog
	J0178166(t).gif	10 KB	Ladders By Mail Brochure	142 KB	Skills Review	
	J0178166.cil	19 KB	Ladder Conversion	112 KB		
			Comix Alive Web Site	106 KB	Independent Challenge 1	Create with Catalog
			Family Newsletter,	142 KB	Independent Challenge 2	Create with Catalog
			Family Web Site	244 KB		
			Joke Shop Web Site	471 KB	Independent Challenge 3	Create with Catalog
			Animated Web Site	87 KB	Independent Challenge 4	Create with Catalog
	Canyon.tif	58 KB	Traveler Web Site	440 KB	Visual Workshop	TIF file inserted into publication
	DSNGRR.tif	51 KB			Visual Workshop	TIF file inserted into publication
Total		185 KB		2908 KB		

Publisher 2000

Glossary

Align To line up objects using the top, bottom, center, left, or right edges.

Animated GIF An image with movement; used in Web pages.

AutoFit Feature that automatically resizes a font and forces text to fit within a frame.

Autoflow Feature that automatically places text not fitting within a text frame into the next available text frames.

Background Behind-the-scenes area of a page used for repetitive objects or text.

Bleed An object that extends beyond a printer's print area that can be trimmed later.

Booklet A publication containing a series of folds or binds.

BorderArt Decorative borders that come with Publisher (or can be created) and can be placed around any object.

Bulleted list Used to illustrate items that can occur in any order.

Catalog Helps create different types of publications.

Clip art Electronic artwork available on your computer.

Clip Gallery Live Microsoft's Web site that continually offers new downloadable images.

Clip Gallery Online artwork organizer in Publisher.

Clipboard Temporary holding area into which objects can be copied and pasted later.

Continued on/Continued from notices Text that automatically tells you where a story is continued on or from.

Copyfitting Makes the copy fit the space within a publication.

Crop Conceals portions of an image.

Design Gallery Formatted elements—such as pull quotes, sidebars, and titles—that can be added to an existing publication.

Design Sets Groups of matching elements in the Design Gallery that contain common themes, colors, or objects.

Desktop publishing program A program that lets you manipulate text and graphics to create a variety of publications.

Dot leaders Dots or dashes that make it easier to read a table of contents or other information.

Drag and drop Moving or copying technique in which an object—or a copy—is dragged to a new location.

Drawing tools Toolbox buttons that let you create geometric designs.

Drop caps A formatting feature that lets you change the appearance of a paragraph's initial character.

Flip Objects created using drawing tools that can be rotated horizontally or vertically using a toolbar button.

Footer Text that repeats on the bottom of each page.

Foreground Area of a page where most information is placed.

Formatting toolbar Buttons on a toolbar that change the appearance of objects within a publication.

Frame Object in a publication containing text, a graphic image, a table, or any combination of these.

GIF format Stands for **Graphics Interchange Format**, and is a commonly used file format for graphics. Used in Web pages due to its small size, this format is displayed *natively* by most browsers, meaning it is displayed without the use of additional programs.

Graphic image A piece of artwork in electronic form.

Group Turns multiple objects into a single object.

Grouping Turning several objects into one, which is an easy way to move multiple items.

Handles Small (usually black) squares displayed around the perimeter of a selected object.

Header Text that repeats on the top of each page.

Home page The first page, or primary page, in a Web site.

Horizontal ruler Measuring guide that displays above the publication window.

Hotspot A hyperlink confined to an area within an object.

Hyperlink Text or graphic that, when clicked, jumps to a new Web page. Hyperlinks Web pages together on the Internet.

Kerning Adjusts the spacing between character pairs.

Keywords Words used to locate images within the Clip Gallery.

Layer Changes the position of objects in relation to one another so that one appears to be on top (or behind) another.

Layout guides Horizontal and vertical lines (on a publication's background and visible on the screen) that help you accurately position objects within a page.

Logo Distinctive shape, symbol, or color that is visibly recognized as belonging to a company or product.

Masthead The banner at the beginning of a newsletter containing its name, volume, issue, and date.

Measurements toolbar Toolbar that lets you more precisely move, resize, or adjust objects.

Menu bar Contains menus from which you choose Publisher commands.

Mirrored guides Layout guides and margins on left and right facing pages that appear to be mirror images.

Numbered list Used to list items that occur in a particular sequence.

Object shadow Gives an object the illusion of depth by adding a shadow behind it.

Objects toolbar Contains buttons used to create and enhance publication objects.

Orientation Position in which the paper is printed.

Pack and Go Wizard Feature that compacts all the files needed by a commercial printing service onto your choice of media.

Page icons Located at the bottom of the workspace, one page icon displays for each page in the publication. Click a page icon to go to a specific page.

Personal Information sets Four distinct sets of information that can be used to store frequently used information such as names, addresses, and phone numbers, that can be placed automatically in publications by the Catalog.

Placeholders Frames created by the Catalog that you can later replace with your own information.

Point size The measurement of the height of a character. 1/72nd of an inch equals one point.

Prepress work Process in which a commercial printer verifies the availability of fonts and linked graphics, makes color corrections or separations, and sets the final printing options.

Proof print Approximation of how your final printed publication will look.

Publication A document created in Publisher.

Pull quote A short statement extracted from a story and set aside from the body of the text.

Reversed text Formatting method that displays light characters on a dark background.

Rotate Changes the position of an object in degrees from a horizontal plane.

Rotation An object's position measured in degrees from a horizontal plane.

Ruler guides Created in the foreground of individual pages by dragging a ruler by holding [Shift]. (Also sometimes referred to as ruler guide lines.)

Rulers Horizontal and vertical scaled displays beneath the toolbars and to the left of the workspace.

Scanner Hardware that enables you to turn information on a paper copy into an electronic file format.

Scratch area Surrounds the publication page and can be used to store elements.

Sidebar Information not vital to a publication placed to the side of the regular text.

Snap To commands When turned on, this feature has a magnet-like effect that pulls whatever is being lined up to an object, a guide, or a ruler mark.

Spelling checker Used to check a story—or the publication—for spelling errors.

Standard toolbar Buttons on a toolbar for completing common tasks, such as saving and printing.

Status bar Located at the bottom of the Publisher window; provides information relevant to the current task.

Story Text in a publication.

Style Defined set of text formatting attributes.

Style by example Names an existing set of text attributes as a style.

Table AutoFormat Pre-existing designs used to quickly format a table.

Table Tabular arrangement of information organized in columns and rows.

Tabs A defined location that the insertion point advances to when [Tab] is pressed.

Text frame Graphic object in which text is typed.

Text overflow Text that does not fit within a text frame.

Title bar Displays the program name and the filename of the open publication.

Toolbars Contain buttons for the most frequently used Publisher commands.

Two-Page Spread View that enables you to see two pages at once.

Ungroup Turns a single object into multiple objects.

Ungrouping Turns one combined object into individual objects.

Vertical ruler Measuring guide that displays to the left of the page.

Watermark A faint, lightly shaded image that appears behind other images.

Web folder A shortcut to a location on a Web server where your pages will reside.

WordArt   An object containing curved or wavy text.

Workspace   The area where a new or existing publication appears.

Workspace page   Contains the currently displayed page.

Zero point   The location of zero on both the vertical and horizontal rulers that can be moved, lets make precise measurements.

Zoom Mode   Makes the page scale larger or smaller to you can move in or away from page objects.

Index

Index

Index

Index

Index